We Are ALL Healers!

Ordinary People with Extraordinary Intention Will Heal the World

Sue Dumais

with guest authors

Marilyn R. Wilson, Kirsten Jorgensen, Nicole McCurdy,
Kim Bergen, Rosemary Laurel Messmer,
Yolanda Sarmiento, Katherine Labelle, Chela Hallenbeck,
Kelli Taylor, Miranda MacKelworth, Kimberley Maxwell,
Aparna Vemula, Julie Ann, April May Bellia,
Jacky A. Yenga, Kristen Bielecki, Kevin Preston,
Surya Devi, and Reverend Lisa Windsor.

Published by Heart Led Living Publishing, January, 2023
ISBN: 9780995813083

Editor: Nina Shoroplova
Typeset: Greg Salisbury
Sue Dumais's Portrait Photographer: Adrienne Thiessen of Gemini Visuals Creative Photography

DISCLAIMER: Readers of this publication agree that neither Sue Dumais nor her publisher will be held responsible or liable for damages that may be alleged as resulting directly or indirectly from the use of this publication. Neither the publisher nor the author can be held accountable for the information provided by, or actions, resulting from, accessing these resources.

This book is a gift for humanity and is dedicated to everyone, everywhere, altogether, all at once.

all my love ♡

Table of Contents

The Healing Power of Presence

The Healing Power of Connection

The Healing Power of Perspective

The Healing Power of Love

How Do You Show Up As A Healing Presence?

The Healing Power of Words

Are You Ready to Embark on a Healing Journey?

I believe everyone is a healer, whether they realize it or not.

Whether you are a garbage collector, counsellor, grocery clerk, pilot, librarian, nurse, mother, holistic practitioner, energy healer, shaman, or fill in the blank, we are ALL healers because we all have the potential to be a healing presence in the world.

The world needs more of us to show up with the intention to foster healing. We can show up as love. We can meet others with compassion. We can support others through empathy.

We need to heal self. We need to inspire others to heal. And we need to heal our planet.

We ALL have the innate ability to heal our own mind and body. We ALL have the potential to be a healing presence for others. AND we ALL contribute to the healing of the whole of humanity and Mother Earth, whether we realize it or not.

The Truth is we are ALL ordinary people capable of having an extraordinary impact!

Imagine if we ALL did that on purpose.

Imagine how quickly the world would change if we ALL said yes to heal our blocks to love and lead with our hearts.

Imagine if we ALL became beacons of light illuminating the path of healing and love alignment for self and others.

Imagine if we ALL learned how to meet fear with love, so that love expands to become the primary force that guides ALL of us in every moment.

Imagine a world where we ALL lived in peace and harmony.

Imagine a world where everyone accepted and honoured our differences and celebrated our uniqueness.

Imagine if we ALL made a conscious choice to see each other through the lens of love, compassion, and empathy.

The world would change in an instant!

That is the vision I choose to hold. That is the world we could all feel proud to live in. That is what is possible if we ALL said YES to be the healer we are meant to be.

Would you like to learn how to become more of a healing presence in your work, in your relationships, and in the world?

The good news is you don't need to leave your job (although some may be guided to). Becoming more of a healing presence is about holding a clear intention and learning how to incorporate simple highly effective healing tools as well as integrating the practice of healing into every aspect of your life including all your interactions with others.

I invite you to join us as we hold the intention to empower each other to heal our wounds of separation and free our minds from fear as we remember and embrace the Truth of who we are, which is LOVE.

You are here reading these words for a reason. Perhaps you feel your heart calling you to do something to contribute to the healing of our planet and humanity.

How can you be more of a healing presence in your life and in the world?

This book is designed as a road map filled with stories, lessons, insights, and tools to empower and inspire you to awaken your innate ability to heal self as you inspire others to do the same.

This book is a healing journey with the potential to create a SHIFT in the collective consciousness from head to heart as we heal our blocks to Love.

This book is a paradigm shift to open our minds to embrace a new Truth that we are ALL healers no matter what we do in the world.

This book is an opportunity to be part of the creative solutions that hold the potential to contribute to the healing of the whole of humanity.

This book is a shift in perspective to change and open our minds to align with the healing potential within each of us as we become a healing presence for everyone in our lives.

This book is filled with a collection of guest authors sharing empowering stories to help everyone awaken to the Truth that there is a Healer in each of us.

This book is an invitation for healers everywhere to evolve, to enliven, and to expand their intuitive gifts.

This book is a catalyst to accelerate the movement to heal the Healers everywhere as they rise up and become more of a healing presence in the world, creating a ripple effect that reaches all corners of the globe and beyond.

This book is a gift for humanity as we instill hope and inspiration through sharing stories and insights that have the potential to uplift humanity, uniting us in love for each other and our planet.

Are you ready to embark on this journey with us and learn how to become more of a healing presence in your work, in your relationships, and in the world?

Let's begin ...

Why Healing? Why Now?

If there were ever a time where we all needed to come together and heal, it is now. Healing offers an invitation for reconciliation within each of us individually and collectively. It is an opportunity to mend our wounds of separation, heal trauma, and forge a path of harmony for all.

I believe we can all agree that the world needs some love and support right now to recover from trauma. Many people are entering a phase of post-traumatic stress from the two years of isolation, uncertainty, and fear from the impact of the pandemic.

We need to put our personal opinions and judgments about the pandemic itself aside for a moment so we can focus on the aftermath of the impact it has left. We can acknowledge that we need to bring some energy to heal around the experiences we endured and the fear that continues to plague many people.

We also need to take a radical, honest look at our shared history and all of the leftover trauma that has been buried and swept under the rug for many years and many generations. We have a lot of history and collective baggage as a society, within our cultures, within our countries, within our ethnicity, and on our planet.

The first instinct would be to run and hide from the mountain of historical collective wounds that are rising to the surface, but that is what we have been doing for years and that clearly doesn't work. Everything is rising to the surface to be revealed and healed whether we want it to or not. We can't bury our heads in the sand anymore, hoping it will all just go away or remain hidden. Ignorance and turning a blind eye are no longer even options.

We have hit a tipping point where healing has become non-negotiable. We have become way more sensitive and our tolerance has lowered to a level that we can no longer pretend, ignore, bury, or hide our leftovers. Everything is like a festering boil coming to the surface to be healed. We can look around and see it everywhere.

At this point, it is exhausting and futile to resist the process of healing that has been activated. It requires way more energy and effort to try and keep things hidden, especially when there are forces working on our behalf to bring it all into the light of awareness to heal.

The first step is to accept the fact that what used to work is no longer working because what used to be tolerated is no longer acceptable.

We can't keep living the way we have been living for many reasons. Mother Earth is calling for us to change. The Universe is calling for us to evolve. We can either evolve as a species where we choose to stand united in love and respect for each other and our planet or we will not survive.

This is not about doom and gloom. It is about taking a radical, honest look at where we are standing at this time in history. It is about learning how to live in harmony with each other and our planet. It is about making a conscious choice to heal all our blocks to love so we can find a new way of being in relationship with each other. A way of living that fosters unity, love, compassion, empathy, harmony, collaboration, cooperation, and creative solutions that serve the whole of humanity and our beautiful Mother Earth.

It is NOT a time to lose hope. I do not believe this is the end. I know in my heart this is a turning point. It is a pivotal choice point and we are all standing on a precipice of potential for a new way of living and being in relationship with each other. At this time, I have more hope for humanity than I have ever had. We are on the verge of a miracle, a SHIFT, an invitation to heal fully, so we can *be the change* as we unite in love for each other and our planet.

Uniting in love is not only possible, it is inevitable. If we all make a conscious choice to heal ourselves and to each be a healing presence to inspire and empower others to do the same, we will create a ripple effect that will reach all corners of the globe.

Are you with me?

Hold steady with me as we explore healing a little deeper.

Take my hand and let's keep going. Say YES! Just say YES!

What Is Healing?

Most people think of healing as a process in the physical body. I see healing as a process of remembering. It is about remembering how to live in harmony with our soul, mind, and body. When we remember how to live in harmony within ourselves and with all of creation, we live with a sense of purpose and our life feels meaningful. For me, healing and harmony are about learning how to honour our humanness and embody our Divinity all at the same time.

The biggest challenge for most people is that they forget that they forgot. They live life by default, believing that life is happening *to* them and that they are victims of their circumstances. When we forget, the mind is split, and the disharmony between our mind and heart causes us to experience more suffering and pain, which ends up being projected onto others as judgment creating conflict, division, and separation. This disharmony can also lead to physical symptoms and dis-ease as well as emotional and mental instability and challenges.

I believe our life is a classroom designed specifically to foster our deepest healing and greatest awakening in the shortest amount of time. It is filled with challenges, obstacles, and opportunities to heal our minds, align our hearts, and evolve our souls. It is designed to help us remember the Truth of who we are, which is Love.

My entire life has been about healing. I believe it is why I am here on this planet at this time, to inspire and empower healing in self and others. I have studied, practised, experienced, and witnessed many forms of healing and I have seen more miracles than I can even begin to count.

As an intuitive healer, I approach healing from a number of different angles, which fosters more of a soul-mind-body approach. Over the years, I have been intuitively guided to explore different approaches to healing the physical body, but I also discovered the importance of healing on all levels including mentally, emotionally, energetically, and spiritually. Each of these paths can also be explored individually and collectively. Our unresolved wounds and trauma can influence our own lives as well as impact the whole of humanity.

The key is to identify where the wound or trauma is rooted. When we can shine light on the root cause, we can unravel the snowball effect it created in the individual. This impacts the whole person as well as contributes to the healing of the whole. The good news is that we don't need to go digging like archeologists and meticulously study each and every root. Sometimes just shining a light on the root can clear it; other times we need to process it emotionally, mentally, and energetically as well. Each layer is different and requires us to be wide open to explore with a curious mindset.

When we remain curious and open, we can approach our unique path to healing without judgment. When we have some basic healing tools in our pocket, we can move through the process more efficiently. We can remain open to receive any insights as well as process any essential emotions or energy that need to be cleared in order to free ourselves fully.

What I do know for sure is that it will take time, energy, and willingness, but it won't actually take as long to heal as we think. Remember there is an energy rising to foster a quickening, and an efficiency for all of us to heal fully and thoroughly without skipping any essential layers.

Where to Begin

How Do We Heal?

I have discovered there is no one recipe that fits all when it comes to healing. There are many ways to heal and thousands of different tools that we can use to assist us. That can be both good news and challenging news at the same time, because it may become overwhelming or confusing to figure out which path to take and what tool to use and when. When we add the often well-meaning advice and recommendations from others, the overwhelming choices can paralyze our mind from taking any action.

Your path to healing may have similarities to others', but your path will be unique to you. We all have our own unique circumstances, upbringing, programming, limiting beliefs, fears, emotions, trauma, triggers, and hidden roots that need to be healed in the way that we need to heal them. We also need to honour the time we need to heal these pieces. Some will be quicker and easier than others. Some require more energy to move through the layers and shine light on the root.

The best way to discern is to trust our own intuitive knowing. The recipe and breadcrumbs to follow for our unique path are seeded in our heart. When we follow our heart, we can bypass the fear-based programming and filters in our mind that can actually block, stall, or distract us from looking within and healing our leftovers.

The heart is unbiased. The heart knows what we need when we need it most. The heart is our best guide.

Even when I receive intuitive messages for my clients, I always encourage them to take the insights and bring everything all into their own heart. The last stop must always be our own heart, because even our own mind can be an obstacle.

Are We Leading with Love or Fear?

Before we continue our healing journey in this book, it is important to understand that our mind is powerful. It can support and propel us on our path of healing or it can hinder, distract, block, and paralyze us.

There is part of us that wants to heal and there is also a part of us that is afraid to heal. This is where it is helpful to explore the concept that we have two teachers in our mind. One that feeds our fear and one that meets us with love. Our experiences in life are determined by which teacher we are listening to.

In every moment we are listening to one of two teachers: fear or love. I have named the two teachers, Ego and Spirit.

Ego is the voice of fear, doubt, and worry. In my book *The Evolution of the Ego*, I talk about how the ego is like an overprotective helicopter parent who will stop at nothing to keep us safe and protected. It uses fear to keep us playing small and hiding our greatest light because it is afraid of the world. Our ego only knows fear and it is the source of our belief in separation.

Spirit is our teacher that represents the voice of love, intuition, and inner guidance. Spirit reminds us of the Truth of who we are and encourages us to be love and to shine brightly in this world.

In any moment, you have the choice of aligning with one teacher or the other, never both. Love and fear cannot lead you at the same time. It is either one or the other.

Most people are controlled by their ego teacher and they buy into the voice of fear. Fear can be paralyzing and it can also be cleverly hidden. For many people, fear is their default setting because it is so deeply embedded in our mental programming.

Healing is not about avoiding fear; it is about finding the most compassionate path and methods to move through and process our fear to free ourselves fully from it. Facing our fears can be challenging but it doesn't have to be as hard as we think. It won't necessarily be easy, but it will be worth it.

When we meet ourselves and others with compassion and empathy, we can heal our fears and unite in love. Love is a powerful force for change and holds great potential for healing. If we make a conscious choice to meet our fear with love, then Spirit can guide us through the fear and out the other side. Never underestimate the power of a choice for love.

It is important to remember that our choices have impact

and hold potential. When we meet fear with fear, fear expands. When we meet fear with love, Love expands, every single time.

So as we move through the layers and explore the roots of our wounds and trauma, remember to choose love over and over and over again. When you meet others and witness their fear, meet them with love and be the compassionate witness so you can be a loving presence as they heal.

Let's all set an intention to meet fear with love and just be wide open to the miracles and potential that intention fosters. I promise if we shift our mind around this, we will feel more empowered as we choose love as our guide.

Healing Our Body

One of the most effective insights that helped open my mind to experience many different approaches to healing was by exploring the idea that we have five bodies that can hold trauma and cause triggers. The five bodies are the physical, mental, emotional, energetic, and spiritual bodies.

For a period of time, I tried to heal everything that came up for me, using my mind. I went to talk therapy, which worked well, until one day it stopped working. I knew I still had stuff I needed to explore and heal, but talking about it wasn't getting to the root. At the same time, my physical body felt so heavy, dense, and painful. My physical symptoms were getting worse and worse and nothing was relieving the pain.

I kept hearing the words "there is something stuck in my body." I just knew I had to go into my body to find it, but I didn't know how. Whenever I would get remotely close to it, I couldn't bring myself into it fully without getting kicked out by my own fear. It wasn't logical. It didn't make sense in my head but the feeling in my body was real. The fear was real. The resistance was real and it was strong. I felt stuck between knowing there was something I needed to heal and feeling completely helpless because I couldn't get myself where I knew I needed to go in order to heal this heavy stuckness.

That was when I found yoga therapy. It provided the path I needed to go through my body to heal my mind. Instead of trying to heal everything by going into my head to make sense of it all, which I know now can be limiting, I could go into the physical sensation in my body and use it as an entry point to explore the layers and shine light on the root.

This particular layer was intense and it provided another significant Spiritual awakening that dissolved one of my deepest fears, one that had plagued me since childhood.

While I was receiving a yoga therapy session, I suddenly felt the deep fear and the need to run for my life. It didn't make sense in my head but the feeling was so real and I could feel my body's stress response kicking into full gear. Every part of me wanted to run out the door, but I was determined to get to the root so I made a conscious choice to turn and face my fear. I felt a wave of courage rising up inside me, preparing me to face my biggest fear and, to my surprise, I suddenly started laughing.

The yoga therapist asked, "Why are you laughing?"

When I went right into the space in my solar plexus where

I felt my biggest fear, there was nothing there. I was laughing because I was running from nothing!

Then it hit me deep in my heart and I started to cry. I realized I was running from myself. I was afraid of myself. I was running from my power because I was afraid of my power. I was afraid of my intuitive gift and the energy and potential it held. I had spent my entire life running from the gift that I was meant to share with the world. Essentially, I was running from my Truth and denying my purpose.

My body started to shake uncontrollably. At first I was embarrassed and afraid, but something about it felt freeing. Instead of stopping or resisting it, I surrendered to it. It was like there was a physical and energetic intelligence that took over and shook the trauma and fear out of my body.

I freed myself from that long-held fear that day and something profound shifted within me. Not only did I heal my mind of that hidden limiting fear but I freed my body, my energy, and my soul. It was my first experience of a full circle healing where I felt the release on every level of my being: physically, mentally, emotionally, energetically, and spiritually.

I left that session with a deep knowing that healing was so much more than just a mental process. We need to take many different approaches and find the one that works for us.

For me going through the body to heal my mind was a breakthrough and it became the foundation of my healing practice. It inspired me to become a yoga therapist and an energy healer. Today I combine all the modalities I have learned to offer more of a soul-mind-body approach.

I was deeply intrigued to learn more about how to use the five bodies as keys to identify where the leftover wound or trauma is rooted or hidden. I discovered it can be rooted in any of the five bodies. It is important to note that if a wound is rooted in the energy body and someone is approaching it solely from the mental body, full circle healing will not take place. If we try to heal the body but don't address the trauma that remains in the mental or emotional root, it will be a temporary fix or bandage.

Although there is often an overlap and the five bodies aren't really separated in the healing experience, using the perspective of the existence of the five allows us to be open to explore physical symptoms from all paths, which can be a key to explore, expose, and heal any hidden roots.

Full Circle Healing

Beyond Physical and Emotional Healing

According to dictionary.com, *healing* is defined as to make healthy, whole, or sound, restore to health; free from ailment.

Most people can relate to the idea of healing when it comes to the physical body. If we cut our skin, our body responds to heal the wound using a complex biological process. The body's first response is to send platelets for clotting and restrict the blood vessels around the wound site to stop bleeding. Then the white blood cells arrive to eliminate any bacteria and keep the wound clean to prevent infection. The body starts to rebuild and repair the damage in the tissues using fibroblasts and collagen as well as building strength in the newly formed tissues around the wound.

Our body has an innate ability to heal and repair itself. We don't need to focus on the cut and tell the body to heal; it just does it naturally. We can assist the body in healing by providing an optimal environment. For example if we have a deep cut on our arm, our body will get to work right away to begin the healing process. If we go to a doctor and get stitches to bring the edges of the wound closer together, the suture thread provides a more optimal environment that can speed up the process of healing and we are less likely to end up with a deep scar. When we keep the area clean and dry we can assist our body in preventing an infection.

Our body wants to be in harmony and when we provide it with the best environment then we can support our body and live harmoniously.

Our body's ability to heal is deeply influenced by the environment in our mind. Our thoughts and beliefs can have a positive influence on healing or they can have a negative impact and block or interfere with our body's innate ability to heal.

Our willingness to feel and process our emotions is also key to providing a healing environment that can support us on every level. We are taught to block or hold our emotions back, to hide them, or swallow them down. Emotions are *energy in motion*. They are meant to be released, otherwise they are held in our bodies as dense energy that accumulates and causes blocks that lead to dis-ease.

Everything is made up of energy. Our body, our thoughts, beliefs, emotions, everything within and around us. It is all energy. Sometimes our trauma is being held or may be rooted in our energy body. Being open to feeling the more subtle layers of energy within and around us can support us in healing fully.

Do We Really Need Healing?

The Truth is we don't need healing. Yes. You read that correctly. The only reason we need to talk about healing is because we believe in our mind that we are broken, damaged, and need to be fixed or healed. We weren't born with those beliefs in our mind; we were programmed and taught to believe those things.

We have been convinced that there is something fundamentally wrong with us. We are constantly bombarded by messages that tell us how we are not enough and that we need to change in order to be loved and accepted. We need to do something in order to feel whole and complete.

Even aging is touted as a problem that we need to prevent or fix. Aging is just a natural process of life. Feeling stressed, worried, or pressured about it will only add years to our physiological age. The truth is when we resist life, hold onto fear and past trauma, bury our emotions, and believe the lies that we are not enough, the burden and pressure of carrying all of that is enough to age us. Trying to live up to the unattainable societal expectations is stressful, exhausting, and painful because it is keeping us separated from the Truth in our heart.

Our minds think we need to be healed because that is what we have been told directly and indirectly. Our minds believe that if we change ourselves, if we heal, then we will be accepted, loved, and feel whole.

Stress, pressure, expectations, unresolved trauma,

unexpressed emotions, limiting beliefs, and a constant state of trying are all forms of resistance; they create disharmony in our body and lead to dis-ease and illness.

Resistance is the gap between what our mind thinks and what our heart knows. When our mind and heart are not in sync, we experience resistance.

The biggest problem is our mind *thinks* it knows, while our heart *knows* it knows. Our heart holds the Truth. And the Truth is we are loved without conditions, worthy beyond measure. We are whole and complete just the way we are.

When we learn to use resistance as a tool to shine light on what we need to heal we can make quicker progress by taking the most direct route to the source of the discord within us. Resistance is a finger pointing us in the direction of what needs to be revealed in order to heal.

What Is a Trigger?

When we feel triggered, we can use resistance as a tool to look within to reveal how to heal self.

Our triggers are fingers pointing to our leftovers, the ones that need healing within us. When we feel emotionally reactive toward someone or to something that is happening, it is our mind and body's way of protecting us from more hurt, attack, or betrayal. Life is bumping up against an unresolved emotional wound within us and we react because we feel the need to protect, defend, or hide it.

A trigger may show up as an emotional outburst of anger or

rage. We may suddenly feel anxious, fearful, restless, irritated, or annoyed. We may recoil, feel like we want to run and hide, feel withdrawn, or even become numb, helpless, powerless, or hopeless. Or we may experience a surge of energy and feel like we need to stand our ground and fight, yell, or scream.

We may even experience the physical expression of the emotional trigger first. Suddenly, we feel nauseous or have a sudden experience or an increase in physical pain, tightness, or tension in our body.

It can often feel as though we are overreacting to a situation or having an uncontrollable knee jerk reaction. I often see it in my clients as a volcanic reaction. The unresolved trauma or wound has been bubbling and rumbling under the surface for a while, often for years or even decades. When the trigger reaction hits, the volcano explodes, surprising everyone around them because no one was aware of the dormant volcano hiding under the surface.

This volcanic reaction often surprises my clients as well, because they didn't realize what they had buried either.

When life bumps up against our leftovers, it is hitting up against an unresolved past trauma or experience that was never fully felt and processed. That trauma remains in our body and energy field as a tender wound or an unresolved grievance that was never fully healed and processed.

The outward reaction, our trigger reaction, is our way of protecting ourselves from getting hurt further or adding more trauma to our unresolved wound. We react out of fear instead of responding. If we recognize our trigger and shift our intention to making a conscious choice to respond instead of react, we can use it to bring about a full circle healing.

A full circle healing happens when we complete the experience or process the emotion or energy that is being held in our mind, body, and/or energy field. If we complete the experience by healing the unresolved trigger, we will experience full circle healing. We will feel resolution, the trigger will dissolve, and we will no longer react.

When we heal it fully, wholly, and completely, we will no longer feel the need to react, defend, protect, or hide because we will feel empowered and capable of responding rather than reacting to life.

We can heal our leftovers on our own, but sometimes our wounds need witnessing. In my intuitive healing sessions, I bring my clients through a guided somatic experience where we go into the body (soma) and explore the energy, emotions, and physical expressions of it.

I share any messages or intuitive insights I receive to help them fill in the gaps. This provides them with a level of understanding for their mind so they can let their wounds go. As a compassionate witness, I create a sacred container and provide a safe space to process the unexpressed emotions. I guide my clients with each step and walk with them into the depth of the wound or trauma and out the other side.

I have guided thousands of clients through extremely vulnerable and emotionally sensitive traumas by holding a space of love, tenderness, and grace. I am able to provide a quickening as I lead them through the expression of the energy of those deeper painful layers in a less painful way and with more speed. I remain in awe of the miraculous shifts they experience when they are freed of the leftovers and experience full circle healing.

So the next time you experience resistance or feel triggered, be open to see it as a finger pointing to a leftover wound. Be willing to explore the idea that you may not be upset for the reason that is in front of you, but because there is something within you that needs to be healed.

Be willing to go within and explore what is underneath your trigger. If you can shine light on the root of your upset, you can heal it.

Feel your feelings, challenge your thoughts, change your beliefs, process your fears, forgive self and others, move through your physical trauma, and meet yourself with love, compassion, and empathy as you move through each layer.

Remember that we will feel capable of processing some triggers on our own, while others may need a compassionate witness and guide. The good news is we can always trust our heart to lead us to the tool, the resource, or the individual that is meant to support us. We don't need to do it alone! Asking for help may feel vulnerable but it is a sign of true strength and courage.

Healing Our Blocks to Love

Why Do We Block Love?

"Your task is not to seek for love, but merely to seek and find all the barriers within yourself that you have built against it."
Rumi

Why on Earth would we block love? What is it about love that would cause us to build up a wall of defense against it? It helps to understand that when I speak of love there are two forms of love available to us: human love and Divine Love.

Human Love

The human version of love in this world is what we are taught to seek and find outside ourselves. It is a version of love that appears to come and go. It is fleeting. It is offered by some and then withdrawn when we do something "wrong." Human love is conditional. It is embedded with guilt, judgment, expectations, and limits. It must be earned and we must be worthy to receive and experience it.

Human love can make you feel alive inside and full of joy and happiness and put a skip in your step. While you may feel like you are skipping on the clouds, underneath there is always a shadow side of love that is riddled with fear, lurking in the background.

For many people, human love is terrifying, full of uncertainty, risky, vulnerable, dangerous, hurtful, and full of potential rejection and profound loss. We are afraid to love fully because we are afraid to lose love. Human love is conditional, so it feels like it can be lost, taken away, or withdrawn. It is a temporary symbol of our connection to others and our attachment to objects, people, or places.

Human love creates a temporary bandage to cover our wound of separation. This wound runs deep within each of us and has generational roots that run even deeper in our subconscious mind.

Separation is a gaping festering wound. At the same time, it can be a hidden silent void that strangles joy, peace, and happiness. The wound of separation can lead us into a loop of perpetual inner seeking and yearning, and at the same time feed our fear, causing us to avoid and/or defend love.

We are hungry for love, yet terrified of it.

We want it and we don't want it.

We grasp for it at the same as we push it away.

We are stuck in a never-ending inner game of tug-of-war in which there is no real winner. We are the one pulling on each end of the rope, fighting against ourselves. It is exhausting, defeating, and we end up feeling stuck in limbo.

This internal disconnect feeds a void that just can't seem to be filled no matter what we do. We may feel a sense of loss. We may feel disconnected and isolated. The pain and suffering of being separated from our true essence is accumulative and debilitating, or it becomes a driving force to do more, achieve more, and try harder as we try to prove our worth to self and others. We lose our self in fear, and block the only thing that can truly free us, Divine Love.

Divine Love

Divine Love is the truest, pure, and uncontaminated form of Love. It is limitless, boundless, and unconditional. It is available to everyone, in every moment because it is our essence. It is our true nature.

Divine Love is difficult to define because it is more of a feeling. It is more of an experience. The moment we try to use words to describe it, we limit it. Divine Love is indescribable. Using our human language to define it is impossible. We also limit our experience of it because we are taught to fear it. Our mental filters and fear-based programming keep most people disconnected from it.

Our biggest wound is the wound of separation. Not only do we feel separated from our true Self, there is also a wedge of separation between each of us. That wedge is fear. We are afraid of our Truth. We have been programmed to fear our essence, which is Divine Love.

So how do we heal our fears, change our minds, and open ourselves up to experience Divine Love more fully again? It begins with a conscious choice to remember the Truth of who we are. To remember we are created by Love, we come from Love, and that we ARE Love. When we set an intention to remember, we can begin to open up to experience our Divine essence. We can make a conscious choice to be "Love in action."

Imagine how different the world would be if we all remembered the Truth that we are the Divine embodiment of Love. Our human experience would change in an instant as we allowed Love to animate us in our humanness. We would be Love in action. We could embrace our humanness while embodying our Divinity. We would remember that we are all connected and share the same Source. We would remember we are all brothers and sisters, and we are ONE with all of creation. We are ONE with everything, everywhere, all together, all at once.

When we heal our blocks to love by exploring all the ways we are afraid of love, we can reprogram our minds, remember our Truth, and fling our hearts wide open to experience the depth of love we are capable of feeling.

And that is a recipe that holds the potential to unite us all in Love.

Healing Roles

What Role Are You Meant to Play in the World?

We each have a role we are meant to play in this world, whether we realize it or not. Every role plays an essential part in the healing of the whole. These roles may lead us to our chosen career, job, profession, or passion. They are actually designed to be guiding lights that give us a sense of direction and alignment with our Soul's mission.

When we are clear about our Soul's Divine mission and the roles we are meant to play in this world, we find the answers to the burning questions "Who am I?" and "Why am I here?"

Before we arrived in this human experience, we chose, volunteered, or were assigned specific roles to play. When we live in alignment and honour our assigned roles, we feel a sense of purpose, clarity, and passion that carry us through all of life's challenges. We feel a driving force of energy that propels us in the direction we are meant to go. We feel on purpose, on point, and on track and we actually have a more profound impact on others.

When we have awareness and clarity about what our roles

are, we will be more of a healing presence for others because it will change how we show up in every aspect of our life. When we show up as a full expression of our true Self and a healing presence for others, we will leave a lasting impression in their heart and impact their life in a positive way.

Let me share a few examples.

There was one local garbage collector who left a lasting impression on me, and to this day whenever I reflect back, the memory brings a smile to my heart. Yes, it was a garbage man who inspired me to reflect on how even the most mundane tasks can bring us joy and purpose, depending on how we choose to do them.

Every week whenever I heard the garbage truck coming down our street, I would go to the window and watch in anticipation, for the acrobatic dancing garbage man. He picked up the garbage cans like an acrobat, swung them around, and dumped them into the truck with such grace, strength, and joy. He had not only discovered a clever intense workout for himself but he was also expressing his creativity through movement and dance. He looked like he was having so much fun doing a job that many would judge as mundane.

My sense is that two of his roles in this world are a Spark and a Beacon. When I witnessed his rhythm and passion, he sparked joy in me. He was a beacon of creativity, playfulness, and fun. He reminded me to have fun and discover how to bring more joy into my own work.

Another individual who left an imprint in my heart was a crossing guard at a local crosswalk for students heading to school. He was at least eighty years old and showed up every morning and afternoon to usher the kids across the road safely. I am not sure how long he was doing that job or if he even got paid for it, but I knew the moment I first saw him that he was no ordinary crossing guard.

I could feel the love pouring from his heart. He was on a mission to touch the hearts of every single person he encountered. He would make direct eye contact with everyone, smiling and waving at everyone, including at every single car that drove by.

My sense is that some of his roles were a Tuning Fork, a Symbol, a Spark, and a Connector. As a tuning fork, he held the frequency of unconditional love and it was palpable when he looked at you. His smile was bright and infectious as he connected with each and every student who crossed the road. His smile and love for everyone was inspiring and created a spark in others to pay it forward. He became a symbol in the community. I was probably not the only one who was sad to drive by one day and see that he was no longer standing guard at his post.

I still feel his loving presence when I drive by that crosswalk and it makes my heart smile to remember how he made everyone feel. It has been four years since I last saw him there, but he left a lasting imprint in my heart and I am sure the hearts of many others.

Some of Our Roles

I was deeply curious when this list of roles came through me as channeled creative content for my Spiritual mentoring program. While the list continues to grow and evolve, I am guided to share some of them here to explore some possible roles we have come here to fulfill.

We can have several roles that are more active and present in our lives, while others may feel more dormant, playing in the background. We can also have certain roles that we play in certain aspects of our life. The roles we play in our personal life may be similar or different than the roles we play in our professional life. Sometimes our roles will also vary within our different relationships. How we show up as a parent may be different than how we show up as a friend, colleague, or family member. Our roles may also change and evolve as we move through life.

As you read through the list be curious and feel into each one. You may resonate deeply in your heart with one or more of these roles. Don't get caught up in how they would translate into form or career or purpose. Just feel into which ones resonate first.

Activator	Creator	Seer
Beacon	Healer	Spark
Bridge	Igniter	Symbol
Catalyst	Lighthouse	Teacher
Channel	Mentor	Transmitter
Connector	Messenger	Tuning Fork
Creative	Observer	Wisdom Keeper

Write down which ones you resonate with. Be deeply curious and wildly open to explore how the roles you resonate with translate into how you are showing up in life, in your work, and in your relationships. I invite you to write or journal about them and see if you can tap into the feeling of purpose they hold for you. See if you can get in touch with your Soul's mission as you open up to discover which roles you are meant to play at this time that will contribute to the healing of the whole.

If you would like to learn more about your Soul's mission as well as the specific roles you are meant to play, I dive deep into this content and provide all the tools you need to get clear in The Healer's Tool Box on my website at www.heartledliving. com.

Now let's explore the one role on this list that is what this book is centred around, the role of a healer.

What Is a Healer?

As I mentioned before, we all have the ability to heal ourselves and to be a healing presence for others. So, yes, it is true that we are all healers. It is also important to embrace the idea that some of us are meant to play the specific role of Healer.

Some of us are meant to be recognized as a healer, like an empath, shaman, or medicine man or woman. I know many physicians and holistic practitioners who are healers and the way they are meant to extend their healing abilities is through their profession.

Some are meant to be playing those professional roles as practitioners with the "healer" embedded into their practice, while some others are hiding behind those more societally acceptable roles when they are meant to come out as healers in the world.

Right now many people are feeling the call to play the role they are meant to play. I am seeing many people changing jobs and leaving their careers to answer the calling in their heart to be healers. Many dormant healers are waking up to recognize that their intuitive gifts are meant to be shared. They are feeling a strong call to make the shift.

In response to the increase in dormant healers waking up or those feeling the call to evolve or expand their intuitive gifts, I created a Spiritual Mentoring Program and Healer's Tool Box specifically to support healers, empaths, and highly sensitive people to activate the full expression of their intuitive gifts. I predict we will see more and more people recognizing they have an essential role to play as healers in the world.

There are different types of healers and empaths and there are also highly sensitive people who may or may not play the role of a healer.

A healer is someone who has the innate ability to channel healing energy, receive intuitive insights or Divine messages, and/or can guide others through healing processes, modalities, or techniques. This can be in person, which may include "hands on" healing techniques, or remotely through distance healing. There are many types of healers and the depth and potential of their healing gifts can vary. A healer may be a shaman, medicine man or medicine woman, spiritual healer, faith healer, energy healer, and the list goes on and on. Many different cultures and tribes have their own name for healers. The important part to discern is that healers often feel deep in their soul that they have a role to play as a healer in their community or in the world.

An empath is someone who is sensitive to the energy of other people, places, animals, and other living organisms, nature, Mother Earth and/or objects in the environment. Their sensitivity may translate into feeling in their own body other people's physical pain, emotions, and other sensations. The feelings and sensations can be intense and can often be mistaken for the empath's own physical pain or emotions. It is essential for an empath to learn how to discern between what is their own pain and emotions and when they are picking up on the energy of others. Many of my mentoring students are empaths who need support to understand how to harness their gifts so they can navigate this emotional world without constantly being bombarded by other people's energy and pain.

In my experience, there are at least twelve different types of empaths and each one has specific challenges to learn to overcome and navigate. For example an emotional empath can sense and feel the emotions of everyone around them. They often feel those emotions in their own heart so learning how to discern and clear those emotional messages is essential. A plant empath can feel and sense the trees, plants, and grass. An animal empath is sensitive to the needs, feelings, and physical ailments of animals. When an empath understands their specific sensitivity they can learn how to use their gift in a way that doesn't wreak havoc on their own physical, mental, and emotional well-being.

It is helpful to understand that many empaths are healers, but not all healers are empaths. Many people who are in the helping profession often have some degree of empathic sensitivities but they are not necessarily meant to play the role of a healer in the world. They are meant to be a doctor, counsellor, or other helping professional. Many artists, musicians, and poets are empaths.

There are many people who are empaths and have no idea. Anyone may be an empath.

I remember the first time someone described me as an empath. It was a huge relief, because I finally understood why I felt the way I did. It was as if in that moment my entire life made sense. Shortly after that epiphany, I discovered I was actually an empath, a healer, and a highly sensitive person.

A highly sensitive person is someone who has a highly sensitive nervous system. They experience heightened physical and emotional sensations and are acutely aware of the subtleties in their environment. They can be sensitive to touch and textures, noises, other people's emotions, electromagnetic fields, Wi-Fi, crowded places, tastes, smells, and so much more. They can experience extrasensory overload in certain circumstances and often find it easier to be in a quiet and controlled environment. They can be sensitive to chemicals, preservatives, and certain foods and can also respond differently from others to medications.

I have described myself as a hyper highly sensitive person. Growing up was intense and confusing because I could feel so much all the time. I felt constantly bombarded and nothing made any sense. Thankfully I have found some technology and tools to support me so I find it easier to function in my everyday life. I have also established a highly effective foundational practice of self-care and soul care, so I don't go into sensory overload anymore. I have learned how to harness and use my sensitivities to enhance my intuitive abilities as a healer and an empath.

It was very confirming when I finally discovered that I am all three: a healer, an empath, and a highly sensitive person. It took many years to figure it all out, but I know now how to honour my gifts, sustain my energy, and navigate my sensitivities.

Some people will be either a healer, an empath, or a highly sensitive person. Some can be all three or maybe just two. It is important to note that most empaths are highly sensitive people but not all highly sensitive people are empaths. Some healers are highly sensitive and some are not. In my experience, it does help others if they know which sensitivity they have or do not have. It is deeply validating and affirming and can give someone a sense of relief when they understand why they feel how they feel.

Are you a healer? Are you an empath? Are you a highly sensitive person? If you have asked yourself these questions before, chances are good that you are at least one of these three.

If you resonate with what I have shared or feel curious to learn more, trust your inner knowing and let your heart lead you to the answers you seek. You may be guided to work with me or someone else to find these answers. You may even find answers to questions you didn't even realize you had.

Remember whether you resonate with calling yourself a healer or playing a role as a healer or not, every one of us has the potential to be a healing presence in the world. You don't need to call yourself a healer if that doesn't resonate or feel true for you, but we can all hold the mindset that our presence is healing. And in that context, we are all healers at heart.

Embracing My Gift as a Healer

I Was Born a Healer

My first memories of being a healer were when I was in my mother's womb. I could hear my parents fighting on the outside and I could feel the emotional impact it had on my mother on the inside. I could feel her anxiety, fear, and worry.

As a child I was extremely highly sensitive. I could feel everything around me. I could feel the trees, plants, insects, animals, Mother Earth, the moon, all of humanity along with all the suffering and pain; I could feel it ALL!

I could feel everyone's emotions in my heart as if they were my own.

I could feel everyone's physical pain in my body as if it were my own.

I could feel so much all the time, and as a child it was intense, heavy, hard, terrifying and, more often than not, it was extremely overwhelming. It was hard to breathe.

I cried a lot. Mostly into my pillow so no one else would hear me. I cried for humanity. I cried for nature. I cried for animals. I felt immense grief, paralyzing fear, extreme pain, and confusing physical symptoms in my body, ALL the time.

I didn't know how to turn it off.

The world seemed so painful and I questioned how anyone could endure this much pain. I asked "why?" a lot, because I wanted to understand how the world worked and why so many people were suffering. It didn't make sense to me. Why would anyone want to live in a world that was so full of pain?

I was deeply confused and conflicted in so many ways. I could sense the good in others, but I could also feel their shadow sides.

I was born with a strong calling in my heart to heal the world. I wanted so badly to help everyone to heal their pain and suffering, so I tried to carry it for them. It was a heavy burden to carry, especially for a child. At the same time, it was a strong calling within me and one that I couldn't ignore it. At times, it was so intense that I questioned whether, if healing the world meant I had to endure this much pain, was it worth it? Each time the answer to that question was always yes, even if that meant sacrificing my own comfort.

At a very young age, I decided that I must be cursed and that I was being punished. I carried the burden and weight of the world's suffering and pain on my shoulders and in my body for a long time.

I tried everything I could to numb it out or stop the pain, but that only led to more suffering. The more I tried to numb out or deny my sensitivities, the more sensitive I became. The more I tried to disconnect, the more disconnected I became from my true Self, from my highest purpose, from my calling.

All of which created far worse suffering within my own mind and body. To top it all off, I accumulated a boatload of guilt because I wasn't helping others as much as I knew I was meant to and I wasn't answering the deepest calling in my heart.

I tried to be normal, to be like everyone else, but I never felt normal. I quickly realized that I wasn't like everyone else around me, so I started to hide my feelings and the pain I felt. It didn't feel safe to share and I became afraid of judgment.

At the time I didn't understand what was happening inside me. It was confusing enough to try to navigate and understand my own inner chaos and feelings. When I tried to make sense of the world around me, it felt like an impossible task.

My own physical pain was buried under layers of other people's pain and emotions.

I didn't really understand what I was feeling in my body. All I knew was that I felt a lot of pain all the time. When I would injure or hurt myself, it felt like the straw that broke the camel's back. My own pain felt magnified with intensity far bigger than the injury or wound on the outside.

There were moments when I could actually sense that the pain was not coming from me, even though I was feeling it in my body. I remember having experiences in which someone would enter a room and I would feel pain in my hip. When they left the room it was as if the pain left with them. A few times I could sense where the pain was coming from and when I focused my attention on the person, the pain would soften inside me.

These moments were fleeting because overall the physical

and emotional pain were like constant thorns coming from all directions. And other people's pains didn't always leave my body when they left the room. In fact, more times than not, it lingered for a long time. Being in a public place was often excruciating and deeply challenging.

That was the perfect storm for suffering all the time. When you add my own inner pain and turmoil to the mix, it became a tangled confusing mess of a rat's nest inside me.

While I felt conflicted on the inside, the world outside was one big contradiction, which led to even more confusion. Sometimes I could hear other people's inner thoughts of suffering. It was confusing because most people who were suffering on the inside were often pretending to be okay or smiling on the outside. They were saying one thing and I could sense they were feeling the opposite on the inside. I became a very good lie detector because I could feel the truth behind the words people were speaking. What they were saying on the outside didn't match how they were feeling inside.

In a way, I was doing the same thing. I was weathering an intense storm on the inside while pretending to be okay on the outside. I didn't want to be a burden to my mother or anyone else. I was also terrified of being judged. I was afraid that, if anyone knew what was really going on inside my mind and body, they wouldn't accept me. If they knew the real me, they would be afraid of me or they would condemn me for being cursed.

I lived in a state of constant fear while experiencing constant pain. That is how I lived most of my childhood.

In my early twenties, after years of abusing my body in an

attempt to numb out the pain, I realized that I was teetering on the edge of life and death. My body was weak, my mind was lost in darkness and despair, and I was on the verge of ending it all.

I found myself at the bottom of the bottle. I had hit rock bottom and I hit it hard. I stood on the edge of life and I knew I had to make a choice or that choice would be made for me. I was lost in the darkness of my addictions, yet in the moment, I could see the smallest light at the end of a long dark tunnel.

This light was calling me like a beacon. It was my deepest heart's calling. I had a vision showing me that I was meant to get lost in the dark so that I could help others find their way back into the light. There was something I was meant to do and I could use my life experiences to empower and inspire others. My personal experiences and challenges allowed me to foster deep compassion and empathy for all who were suffering.

I felt a renewed sense of purpose as I reconnected to the calling in my heart to heal the world. This was the catalyst that sparked the willingness and determination to find my way back home to my heart. I knew in that moment that I needed to heal myself so I could help others heal.

Healing Myself

As I took the steps I needed to take to heal myself, I was focusing on helping others at the same time. Every time I helped someone else heal, I was helping myself heal. Every time I healed myself, I seemed to be able to help others even more.

One day when I was sitting with a friend, I could feel a

heaviness fill my heart and abdomen. This time instead of being afraid of it, I softened my mind and became deeply curious for any message it held. I was immediately pointed to my friend. I could sense something inside her that felt darker and denser than everything else. I asked her if she had pain in the area I was sensing and she said yes. I asked if I could try something to remove it and she said yes.

I placed my hand above the area of her body where I could see and sense the density. It was like I reached into her body with my hand, grabbed a hold of it, and pulled it out. Immediately her eyes popped open and she said, "What did you do?"

My first response was to shrink and recoil in fear that I had done something wrong. When she said, "The pain is gone," I felt my courage rise up; I told her, "I removed it." It felt like a miracle for both of us. Her pain never came back.

In that moment, I experienced a profound Spiritual awakening and my life changed in an instant. I saw a light fill my entire being and my mind expanded to create an opening for a new way of being in life. I had a vision of placing my hands on others and helping them heal their pain and suffering. Everything suddenly made sense. I realized that my ability to feel and sense other people's physical and emotional pains was not a curse; it was actually my greatest gift. It was a gift that I was meant to share with the world.

I felt a force of love surround me, igniting a spark within my heart and inviting me to stop hiding. In that one instant, I said yes to play my part in the healing of the whole of humanity and I took the first step toward owning my gift as a healer.

I had no idea how I would do that but I felt a deep trust rising in me. I decided that if I was born with this gift to heal, then the rest of the recipe that provided the "how" had to be seeded in my heart as well. I made a commitment to follow my heart even when it didn't make sense in my head. Somehow I knew and trusted that, if I followed my heart, it would lead me with every step.

Step by step, bread crumb by bread crumb, one ingredient at a time, my life as a healer unfolded.

I challenged all the thoughts I could hear in my head. I committed to changing the limited fear-based programming in my subconscious mind. I gave myself permission to feel all my unexpressed feelings to free myself from my past trauma. "Feel to heal" and "reveal to heal" became my mantras. I learned how to discern between my own pain and emotions and what belonged to others. I became a full-time student committed to living a life of healing and awakening to the Truth.

I became a student of healing. I learned. I read. I studied. I practised. I experienced. I immersed myself fully and I committed to healing everything within me so I could be a clear channel to support others to heal.

When I made the conscious choice to say YES to leading with my heart, to heal myself and to become the healer I knew I was meant to be, everything started to fall into place. I felt a deep sense of purpose and my path was illuminated to reveal the next step. It wasn't easy, but it was worth it.

My personal life and my professional life continuously overlapped and everything fell under an overarching umbrella of healing. I also discovered I had a passion for teaching and empowering others by imparting knowledge to help open and heal their mind.

My intuitive gift continues to evolve and today it allows me to take complex ideas, lessons, and spiritual concepts, and simplify them in a way that the mind can accept and understand. As I work with the energy in the background, it creates a felt experience in others to bring a deeper understanding and integration into their mind, body, and soul.

While I am a spiritual teacher, mentor, and coach, I hold the clear intention to always be a student first. That allows me to constantly evolve and fine-tune my intuitive gifts. My senses have become highly acute, laser sharp, accurate, and profoundly transformative. I am honoured to be a beacon of light illuminating the healing path for others. I have spent the last thirty years healing, teaching, training, and empowering thousands of people. I am passionate about providing advanced mentoring to accelerate and unlock the intuitive gifts of healers, empaths, light leaders, holistic practitioners, and conscious souls all around the globe. I have created a curriculum that brings all my years of experience, practice, and knowing into the classroom to facilitate a quickening and acceleration to fast-track the process of healing and awakening for others.

Our healing process is not about bypassing past traumas,

emotions, or layers within us that need to be witnessed, processed, and healed. It is about clearing all the clutter in the most efficient way and recognizing what needs to be consciously processed and what doesn't. It is about exposing and shining light on what we need to heal, especially the cleverly hidden blocks, and processing it all in the most efficient way. It is about learning how to discern between what is ours and what is not.

Over the last five years, I have received a recurring message during meditation saying, "You are meant to be one of the most powerful healers on the planet at this time." The first time I heard these words, my heart leapt with deep resonance and Truth. I had goosebumps all over my body and felt a huge heart YES. Then I spent years struggling to find a way to embrace these words without fear paralyzing me or ego highjacking it. I wondered how I could say YES to answer that calling, while also remaining humble, without feeling somehow superior or better than others, which is Spiritual Ego.

I would completely let it all go and dismiss it altogether because it felt too big or impossible to align with, without ego coming in to make me feel special. It was actually during the process of writing this book that I finally found a way to reconcile it in my mind. I was given the message to reframe it as "I am meant to play a role as one of the most powerful healers at this time." Embracing it as a role I am meant to play removed my ego from the struggle altogether.

I could feel an authentic heart YES to fully align with

the profound impact and potential this role holds for me, for humanity, and for our planet. Then I was shown that everyone has the potential to play this role, because anyone can set an intention to be the most powerful healing presence they can possibly be. This shift in perspective was exactly what I needed to align my mind, heart, and soul; now it feels inclusive and no one person is more special than another. I have a strong calling in my heart and a deep knowing that I have a significant role to play in supporting humanity to heal so we can unite in love. I have received many visions of what is possible for us, and my faith in humanity is strong. In fact, it has never been stronger than it is right now.

My intention for this book is to empower and inspire all of us to heal. To heal self, to support others to heal, and to each be a healing presence in this world. Together, we can heal all our blocks to love, and own the unique gifts that are seeded in our heart.

After reading this book I believe you will see the Truth that You are a healer! And the world needs you to be a healing presence. Humanity needs all of us to say YES to embody the healer within, so we can all be beacons of light and messengers of love. The world needs you now more than ever. It all begins with saying YES!

What do you say?

Are you willing to say YES and let your heart lead you to the life you are meant to be living now?

Are you open to play the roles you are meant to play now to contribute to the healing of the whole?

Start with YES. Just say YES and see what happens.

Healing through Storytelling

I would like to turn the focus now to letting others share their stories about how they are healers and/or a healing presence for others in their life. I find that it is helpful to hear from more than just one voice and to hear these stories from a variety of individuals with a variety of experiences. These are voices that represent diversity to spark a deep resonance within your heart as you open your mind even more. When we hear other people's stories, we can find common ground, reminding us we are more connected than we are separate.

I share some of my own reflections and insights in and around these stories to weave them together like a beautiful tapestry designed to inspire you to embark on your own inner journey of self-discovery and reflection.

I invite you to keep the following questions in your awareness as you read each story. You may be inspired to record your answers in a journal.

- What stood out for you in this story?
- What resonated for you?
- How did this story inspire you or cause you to pause and reflect on your own life?
- Did you feel triggered by any aspects of the story? (Remember triggers are fingers pointing to what you need to heal within yourself.)

Now let's continue our healing journey together as we connect to ourselves through witnessing the journey of others.

The Healing Power of Words

I am honoured to introduce you to my first guest author, Marilyn R. Wilson. I am sure people who aren't sure whether they are a healer, or don't really relate to the label of "healer," will relate to her story. Marilyn shares a unique perspective around using the power of words to heal, but she also really struggled with the idea of calling herself a healer.

Marilyn's Story

How did words become such a huge part of my life? I can only say it was meant to be. From the time I was young I had two goals: to write the next great science fiction series and to become a counsellor helping people who were hurting to heal. Somehow they both came together.

Growing up in a very strict religious setting, I was insanely interested in how people who didn't fit the mold lived their lives. I didn't fit in and my soul was crying for freedom. What I learned over the years changed both how I looked at myself and where life has led me. In the end, the life that awaited me turned out to be far more wonderful than I could ever have imagined.

As I grew, I dropped the idea of writing a novel, but held tightly to the vision of helping those who were truly suffering. To do that, I first needed to earn my Master's Degree in Counseling. However, my unrealistic dreams of what it meant to be a healer fell to pieces the day my graduate professor, who was also in private practice, shared openly how challenging this career was. Two people he had been counseling had committed suicide that year alone, plus many long-time patients with issues not easily addressed. It was not the idealistic vision I held of being the ultimate healer who magically solved everyone's problems in an hour and sent them on their way.

I found myself lost and adrift. What was I to do with my life now? What was my purpose? I would be fifty before the answer arrived. With my kids older, I was looking for something new to challenge myself. On a whim, I answered an ad from a fashion magazine looking for submissions. I was honestly shocked when two of my submissions were accepted. I had absolutely no writing experience or paper credentials, but from the moment I conducted my first interview, my life hit the accelerator pedal. My soul literally sang during interviews and I was often covered in goosebumps. I just didn't realize at the time what it all meant.

Interviewing turned out to be not only my passion but it also embraced all the quirks society told me I needed to change. These quirks, such as my racing mind so I could think ahead while also listening? Check. An incredible desire to hear people's stories? Check. Making a difference in their lives? Check.

All those I interviewed asked for was a published magazine article promoting their work. How easy is that? People intimately shared their lives with me, which scratched my itch, and in return they received the publicity they desired.

After several years of listening, I was stunned to suddenly become aware of how listening to others had changed how I experienced my inner self and my outer world. Those goose-bump moments, which I thought noted something to be aware of for my article, were actually words of wisdom meant for my benefit. Each was like a pebble dropped in my soul's pond, creating ripples of change within. I started to look forward to these moments with great curiosity. The power of words to create healing and change became real for me on a very personal level over the next few years as listening helped me change from caterpillar to butterfly.

Then came another aha moment that took my passion, my purpose, to a higher level. It was my privilege and joy to give wings to these stories and the powerful lessons they held, by offering them to readers globally through my writing. I realized I had become a conduit for healing on a personal level, and that healing had the potential to bring about incredible change. I realized in that moment that I AM who I am meant to be. There are no mistakes. What a gift! I am filled with gratitude.

When I accepted the offer to write on healing for this book, there were several new moments of clarity that took me by surprise. I began to realize some of the messages I was sharing were lessons from my heart. Not only was I a conduit for the wisdom of others, I was now also giving wings to life lessons of my own. I also became aware that though my first life goal had been to become a counsellor, to heal those who were hurting, I had never considered myself a "healer." Yet here I was answering the call of the universe to offer healing through the power of words.

Does that make me a healer in my own unique way? There have been many moments of wakefulness in the wee hours as I turned this new question over and over. I still don't have the answer, although the mist is slowly clearing and I am beginning to see a vague hint of where I am being led. If I am being honest, what the answer will be does scare me as I struggle to envision calling myself a healer.

In this moment, I choose to simply stand strong in my belief in the power of words—to uplift, to educate, to inform and, yes, to heal. I choose to acknowledge the power of the words I share to create change on a personal and global level, and to embrace this purpose fully in my writing. I also recognize my heart's call to be open to where my journey may lead me next. I stand willing.

How amazing it was the day I finally learned that all the traits making me uniquely me have a life purpose. It took time to find the right garden to plant my seeds in. Once found, my passion matured, allowing me to become a vessel, a conduit, a sharer, and an encourager, giving wings to wisdom and, best of all, offering words to help others heal. I can't imagine a higher purpose than improving the lives of others.

Whether a gift of words bubbles up from the depth of your being, comes to you while you listen to someone speak, or is given to you while reading—know the power of words to heal is immense. Words of wisdom, words of healing, words of acceptance, words of love—they all are at hand ready to support you on your journey. You only have to listen.

I love how Marilyn shares her journey from feeling as though she didn't fit in, to finding her own unique path that allowed her to fulfill and blend her desires to help others heal with finding her passion for writing. I can really relate to the feeling that I don't belong. I struggled with that for a long time.

I am also excited to hear how Marilyn discovered a new perspective that would allow her to embrace the idea that she is a healer, by changing the definition of "healer" in her mind. And she has found her own unique way to be a healing presence in the world.

Words carry a lot of weight because there is so much meaning, history, and energy tied to them. How words land or impact us depends on our beliefs, our culture, our past experiences, and the meaning we place on them individually and collectively. There are many factors that influence how words can impact us and one word can hold completely different meanings for different people.

Words can be used to do harm, because they hold the potential to tear us down, feed doubt and fear as they take the wind from our sails, leaving us feeling stuck or powerless. But words also hold the potential to lift us up and be a source of inspiration, empowerment, and encouragement. When we practise awareness and pay attention to the words we use and how they impact others, we can be a healing presence for others through the written or spoken word. We can use the power of words to heal as Marilyn was inspired to do in her life. The last sentence really resonated for me; the words "You only have to listen" landed deep in my heart.

The Healing Power of Listening

I am honoured to introduce you to Kirsten Jorgensen. The art of listening is a powerful tool and it holds profound potential for healing. Listening and helping others feel heard is an incredible opportunity to foster healing and deeper connections. If we all learn how to listen more, our relationships will be rich and full of love, compassion, and empathy. If we all listen more deeply to our own inner knowing, the world will be a very different place.

Kirsten's Story

Looking back on my childhood I don't really remember how well I listened, but I do recall how it felt when someone really listened deeply to me. I felt heard, accepted, understood, embraced, and seen. It felt like a warm hug. The act of someone else listening to me was healing.

Listening requires silence and space. Many people are afraid of the silence. They are afraid of where it will take them and whether they will come back from it. They are afraid to sit with someone and just be with them. No words. No actions. Just be. I grew up with caring parents in a happy home and my grandparents next door. I remember sitting with my grandpa, just being present and comfortable in the silence together. I felt connected to him even without the exchange of words. We would both be sitting there, twiddling our thumbs, and I loved those moments. Just being together left such an imprint because I could feel the love. I was listening to the energy behind his presence and it felt like such a gift. We were listening without words. We were listening to the silence speak and it spoke volumes in my heart.

As a child, I learned to follow the rules and do as I was told—it was expected. If my emotions were not comfortable for others I was told to keep them to myself. This pushed me away from my feelings and inner knowing, and disconnected me from my heart, sending me into my mind. I stopped trusting my own inner knowing and I stopped listening.

My healing path has been a series of moments that remind me how important it is to listen. To listen to my heart. To listen to my gut. To trust my intuition. To feel my emotions again and to use them as a guiding light to heal and be fully present.

As a young adult, I travelled Europe alone. Looking back on that trip, there were many instances when I listened to that niggling in my gut. It guided me. Decisions on whether to engage or not with others or to go into certain areas or not was like having an internal compass that kept me safe.

As I have been walking my path of healing, I have come to embrace the silence. I am able to sit and be with all states of emotion for myself and others. With my kids, I can sit and witness a tantrum. I can sit with someone in sadness, in joy, in anger, and in fear. I can just be present, listening with all my senses, not just my ears.

Over time, I have come to understand people don't always want an answer or a solution but rather someone to just listen and be there for them. Open. To sit without speaking, to be in the silence together is a gift that holds great potential for healing and connection. I am not scared of the silence, but rather I welcome it fully.

I have found raising children to be a powerful classroom in which to practise being present, listening deeply. The trick for me is to listen without judgment. To listen without trying to impose my own agenda or personal preferences. Being able to set aside my own judgments and agenda allows me to listen to the spoken word as well as the subtle energies behind the words.

When I come to a full stop and truly listen, my children feel my presence and we shift into connection. They feel heard and seen. It is in these moments when I am deeply present that things tend to flow more smoothly.

When I listen with my "busy mom's" distracted ear, I am not fully present and the disconnect leads to moments that bring out explosions and resistance. It sounds like a simple practice but it is not easy. This is still a full-time practice for me and my children. As I continue to meet them with an open heart and hold space to just listen, it becomes easier. The impact it has fostered has led to some of the most rewarding moments for me as a mother.

For as long as I can remember, it fills my cup to listen to others and be a witness to their stories. I feel this is one of the reasons I followed a path into the field of nursing. Through my work as a nurse, I have the opportunity to practise the skill of listening. I get to listen to clients as they express their needs, feelings, frustrations, and progress. The field of nursing is vast but one of our guiding principles is helping others. Being a caring presence in someone's most vulnerable times—times of pain, injury, hurt, love, and joy—is amazing and special.

There is always so much to do as a nurse caring for others: procedures and policies to follow that guide our practice, and tasks and checklists to get completed. But a huge part is listening. Active listening. Listening to their stories, to their hidden subtle gestures—be they physical, mental, or emotional. Being able to tune in and be present can help build deep connection and trust that allow my clients, in their most vulnerable moments, to feel safe enough to share and work alongside me as a member of their care team.

I am always amazed at the healing potential that arises when someone can be fully present and make you feel heard, seen, and accepted. I am equally amazed by the potential that comes from listening to the silence within. I feel so blessed to have listened to my inner voice that guided me to become an intuitive coach and led me to start Peaceful Present Parenting, my online intuitive coaching business. When I trust my intuition and listen deeply to my heart, I am guided in the most miraculous ways. I have learned that my inner voice is guiding me in ways that support me and everyone around me.

Peaceful Present Parenting is about me showing up as an intuitive coach who listens to my inner knowing to guide the sessions. I listen with my inner ear to delve into what my clients need. I listen to them using all my senses—I listen to their words, energy, emotions. I bring everything into my awareness and blend it with my inner knowing to ensure my client gets what they need in that moment. This may be well received or resisted. But if it is guided, I trust it is meant to be shared.

Listening is a practice that at times can sound simple but may not always be easy. The practice of listening that leads to my own healing as well as the healing for others is a practice I am committed to.

Through my journey of connecting with others, I have been witness to healing that comes from just being. Being present to the words, the silence, and the energy. I am always honoured to be a witness to the words and silence that make others feel heard.

Over the years of doing my own healing, I have felt the potential and personally experienced the power of being held in the healing presence by someone who could hold that sacred space for me. And I truly love being a healing presence for others. More recently I have also come to see and embrace myself as a healer. To me, being a healing presence and being a healer are the same. By being a healing presence for self and others, we are all healers.

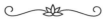

I love the image of Kirsten sitting on the porch with her grandfather feeling such deep love and connection without words. It reminds me of my grandparents and the unconditional love they extended to me. Their love felt so pure and powerful that words weren't necessary, yet they always found the words to express their love as well.

Our presence impacts others way more than we realize and listening deeply to others is such a gift. As a society, we underestimate the power of listening. We are so programmed to think, analyze, and figure things out that we forgot how to be in the present moment. As a newborn or a young child, we were very present, curious, and full of wonder. We listened to the world within and around us. We observed everything because our minds were open and free. As we became adults, we forgot how to listen and how to be present because we were programmed to forget we are intuitive beings and to be in our heads.

May Kirsten's story spark an awakening of your inner child and inspire you to remember how to listen to the silence, and to speak and practise the art of deep presence and wonder once again.

The Healing Power of Animals and Nature

I would like to introduce you to Nicole McCurdy and her journey to discover the power of healing with animals. I have always felt a deep connection to animals and found a sense of home in nature, so I can really relate to Nicole's story of discovering her purpose and finding her voice through the healing power of animals.

Nicole's Story

I am a healer and I am severely dyslexic, easily distracted, and extremely sensitive to everything around me. Never in a million years did I think I would be writing part of a book.

I was the little girl who struggled in school. Growing up, I never felt as though I belonged. I always felt different and making friends did not come easily to me.

I found my sense of peace and belonging in nature and around animals. It is a soft place to land. It is my comfort zone. At the time, I didn't realize just how much healing I experienced being around animals and in nature.

For as long as I can remember, I wanted to be a singer and a veterinarian. I couldn't pronounce "veterinarian," so I used to tell everyone I wanted to be a vegetarian. Singing made me feel alive inside. I would sing all the time. I would hum along or sing a song and make up the words just so that I could keep singing. There was always some kind of sound or vibration coming through me. It was comforting and made me feel calm.

One day, my husband at the time, told me that I would never be a singer because I was no good at it. He told me not to sing anymore, so I stopped singing and something inside me died a little that day. By the time I was twenty-eight-years-old, I was divorced with two young boys.

Determined to embrace my new role as a full-time single mom with no job, I came up with a plan to start my own cleaning company. I wanted to make sure I could be there to drop my kids off at school and pick them up at the end of their day. I was blessed with another baby boy at the age of thirty-four. At that point I needed to make some changes so I could continue to earn money while being at home with a newborn. I expanded my business and started to employ and empower other women. To my delight my cleaning company was taking off, and we were fully booked, servicing many homes.

Around that time I was deepening my journey of self-discovery and healing. I started having memories washing up of past trauma, and I knew I needed to reach out for support. I didn't feel I needed to work with someone in the traditional way. I had already had years of talk therapy. I needed something deeper that included nature, movement, and animals, and that felt more authentically in alignment for me.

I was having dreams about horses. It was as though they were calling me. In my meditations, I kept sensing a deep call in my heart to heal with horses. I didn't know whether there was such a thing, but I knew my heart was leading me somewhere. The next thing I knew, I had hired a mentor. Being on her land and working with the horses spoke to my soul on a very deep level. Little did I know how much my life was about to change.

During my very first session with the horses, I didn't feel anything. My mentor was asking me questions and pointing me in different directions; I had no awareness or insights coming in. When I left the ranch that day, I thought, this is bullshit.

But, obviously something shifted within me, because I went back for more.

After one of our sessions, my mentor asked me if I was interested in training to do what she did. I thought she was off her rocker. How could someone like me do what she did? I was scared and didn't think that I could partner with horses and offer healing sessions for others. Yet I agreed to take the training.

During the training, I had to experience healing my own trauma. I remember one of the sessions where it was my turn to go into the round pen with one of the therapy horses. We were doing a reflective activity and he didn't want to move, so I stood beside him connecting our hearts. I started to feel a lot of emotion rising inside of me, but I didn't want to release it. I was holding onto it. The horse knew what he had to do to help me feel, so he reached over and bit me gently on the arm. I heard the words "lean on me," so I draped my body across his back. As I did that, the tears and emotions started to flood through me and they just kept flowing.

He held me in such a tender, non-judgmental way, while surrounding me with love and light. After twenty-five minutes of him holding space for me, I had moved through all of the emotions. He gently nudged me and walked away. He turned his bum toward me and grounded me in the new energy.

That is when I truly knew through my experience that horses have the ability to hold the space and support healing on a much deeper level than I had ever felt before. It was one of the biggest shifts I have ever had and I am forever grateful for him as my teacher.

I have had many heartfelt experiences with these majestic beings. Sometimes I know exactly what they are saying and sometimes it's just a beautiful sense of energy that washes over my body and releases anything that no longer serves me.

I have had the honour of witnessing some of the most powerful sessions as well when I stand and hold the space with my herd as clients move through their own trauma and emotions. While we are in session, it is not just the horses that come to support the healing. Sometimes, a chicken, a bunny rabbit, a bird, or a plane goes over us. Everything that comes into the one-on-one session is significant and for the client's highest good. One of our favourite sayings when working with horses is you can't make this shit up. Horses are beautiful mirrors for us humans; they show us how to move with grace and ease and allow the flow.

I also started to find my singing voice again

through working with the horses and meditation. When I started working with my clients offering tabletop sessions for healing, I discovered that my voice was ready to be shared with the world again. It started soft and slow as I was having a hard time trusting and working through my own stuff around my voice.

As I deepened my healing and let go of my resistance, I learned to embrace the beautiful vibration and sound that would come out of my mouth. I realized I am a sound healer.

I have started offering sound healing, and I love the connection that I am receiving with myself and my clients through using my voice. It's been a true gift. I am forever grateful to myself, to my herd, and to my clients who embrace me for who I am and allow me to share this beautiful gift that comes through my voice.

So here I am today in a loving relationship with my partner, three amazing boys, two dogs, five cats, forty-plus chickens, and six horses while living on 9.6 beautiful acres of land in Langley, British Columbia. I am a certified intuitive coach, a horse-guided healing practitioner, and a sound healer.

I can honestly say I am proud of myself. It has not been easy, but it has been worth it. No matter what you are going through or the challenges you have had to face, I encourage you to not let anyone take your power away. Your voice matters. Your presence has an impact on others whether you realize it or not. You are incredible and a true gift. May you travel along your journey and shine your light as brightly as you possibly can.

There are so many things in Nicole's story that I can relate to and resonate with. As a young child, my nickname was "Squeak," because I was the shy little girl hiding in the corner of the room afraid to speak. The world was overwhelming to me and I also found solace and peace in nature and among animals.

Animals hold no judgment. Our pets can teach us to love without limits or conditions. My two Chihuahuas follow me around, waiting for me to sit down so they can curl up on my lap. They look at me with deep adoration; I can feel the love in their eyes. It is heartwarming and heart melting at the same time.

Nicole's journey to rediscover her voice and to find the courage to use it as a tool in sound healing sessions for her clients is inspiring. So many people are afraid to share their voice because we are conditioned to be afraid of judgment. We don't even have to use words; we can use instrumental sounds, hum, and employ other vocal tones. Even silence can speak volumes if we really listen.

Whether we are meant to sing a song, speak on stage, write a book or blog, share an inspiring video message, or just offer some insights to a friend or family member, our voice holds great potential of healing for ourselves and others.

The Healing Power of Change

I am honoured to introduce you to Kim Bergen who used to be my dental hygienist. In the last few years, Kim has made some big changes in her life and has used these transitions as a classroom for healing and awakening her hidden intuitive gifts. Many people are feeling a restless stirring inside their soul and feeling called to make big changes in their lives. Some are leaving relationships, quitting jobs, and changing careers altogether, moving out of the city or finding a home in another country.

Kim's story can inspire us to embrace change and trust our own intuition even when others are projecting and feeding fear, doubt, and confusion. We can hold steady in our own inner knowing and embrace the healing power of change.

Kim's Story

I believe healing means easing the suffering caused by past traumas, issues, arguments, programming, and illness. These cause small and big "wounds" that create a path of how we live our life. The wounds can be visible or subconscious. Depending on how big they are, they can cause paralysis on certain paths. Healing is the active form of removing these wounds in order to live a life that we love. A life that brings us home to love, so we can feel more alive.

Am I a healer? I hear a "YES" when I ask my heart that question, but in my logical ego mind, I have never considered myself a healer.

I am in the middle of a big transition in my life right now and on a path of deep self-discovery. Maybe I have always been a healer. Is now the time to embrace this gift? I don't know. All I know is that I have always felt a calling to surround people in loving energy. I love to help them feel better and to create space where they feel cared for.

I have noticed in my lifetime that people seem to like being around me and my energy. People have told me I make them feel comfortable and loved, they feel safe to share things with me, they feel better after spending time with me. I have felt my heart expand in hearing this.

This helped me in my twenty-five-year career as a dental hygienist. Every dental office I worked at, people requested to see me. I believe that was because they felt good after having me clean their teeth, not just from the action of cleaning but from the overall feeling.

I've had people come in with headaches who left feeling better than when they arrived. I used to joke around that "I put love in my instruments." There was so much truth in that because I would feel the love in my heart travel through my arms and into my clients. I would wish them peace, joy, and love. If this is being a healing presence, then I guess I am a healer.

After twenty-two years working as a dental hygienist, something began to feel different. I no longer loved going into work but I still loved serving people and taking care of their teeth. Even though I could feel something was brewing inside, I kept unhappily working at a dental clinic. I was ignoring that inner nudge when my body kept reminding me it was time to make a change.

First, I got a nasty virus that kept me exhausted for many weeks, making me drag myself into work. Then one morning, as I was getting ready, I stood up and got an extreme pain in my lower back. It was so painful that I actually passed out in my bathroom. When I look back at pictures of myself during this time, I look awful: grey and tired.

When I stopped to tune into my heart, I was inspired to start my own holistic dental hygiene care centre. This would enable me to care for patients in a way that felt right to me without being restricted by the confines of the dental clinic paradigm.

I finally gave notice at my job and felt some improvement. I offered to continue working in the clinic for a few months to help them out while I was setting up my own business. It didn't take long until my body, in its final effort to convince me to move on, experienced the worst allergy season ever. I was miserable for weeks. It was like my body kept sending me messages but I would not listen, so it upped the discomfort.

That whole experience was about learning to listen to my body because I couldn't hear my intuition yet. I have since learned to hear my inner voice that guides me to follow my heart. I now actually ask my heart what I am meant to do in all situations in order for me to fulfill my soul's purpose in this life's journey. This quiet voice gives me guidance in each present moment.

I am so grateful I was finally able to hear the guidance to start my own business and give birth to The Happy Hygienist. I opened my doors in the summer of 2018, and I was the happiest I had been in all my years of working as a dental hygienist.

I created a sanctuary where people could come and feel truly cared for. My schedule allowed for time for me to connect with each client, with no rushing in between appointments. I had felt in dental clinics that I could not give my patients all they needed when time was based on production only. As a holistic practitioner, having time to foster deep authentic connection with genuine conversation is super important in creating space for clients to feel safe. In that environment, people can heal in more ways than one.

Then the pandemic happened. Suddenly we all had to stay home, giving us time to reflect and turn inward. It made me stop and take time to re-evaluate my life. One day on social media, I read the words, "If you are meant to leave, now is the time. Everything you now experience will not remain." This message felt like it was speaking directly to me in such a loud way that I couldn't sleep that night.

I asked my heart whether we were meant to sell our home in the mountains. I heard the words, "It is time." The next morning I told my husband we should sell our house and he was shocked. He had been wanting to sell and move for a long time, but I wasn't ready because my daughter was in high school and I did not want to uproot her. I have always been a gypsy at heart and having a child slowed that urge in me as I wanted to create some stability for my daughter. That night lying awake I realized that my daughter was going off to university so I didn't need to stay any longer.

The start of my transition was in the spring of 2021. My husband and I sold almost everything, including two properties and most of our belongings. We bought a travel trailer and in October we started our adventure to drive across the country from British Columbia to Nova Scotia. My daughter had started university there and I was drawn to the East Coast charm, as well as the inexpensive property prices.

My husband and I were being called to get back to basics and to create a little sanctuary where we could be self-sustaining. We found our dream property with over eleven acres on the water. It was a little piece of paradise where we could set up a farm and watch the sun set over the ocean every night.

So many dreams started to come to life. The potential and possibilities were endless, including growing a huge garden of vegetables, medicinal herbs, and fruit trees, and raising many animals to provide food and love.

After twenty-five years of living with my heart

wholly and fully committed to my career as a dental hygienist, something has shifted inside me. I have come to realize that it is not about the actual business; it is about the people. It is about feeling the authentic connections with others that creates the expansion in my heart. I know now that I don't have to be a dental hygienist to be a healing presence and share love.

In this transition of pondering and tuning into my heart to discover what I feel guided to do with my life, another dream opened up. I felt drawn to the healing energy of horses. Their presence is nurturing, grounding, and healing. I received a vision of working in partnership with these gentle creatures to provide a healing experience for others in nature, surrounded by the love of Mother Earth on our beautiful farm. I do not know when my horse partners will show up but I already know that my farm dog Luka—as well as our goats—will be serving with me. Especially our goat Tulip, who seems to have a direct connection to my heart.

I recently completed a six-month course to become a Horse Guided Healing Practitioner and explore the possibilities on our land, creating a healing sanctuary for humans, animals, and the earth.

As I write these words, I am not sure how this will all come about, but I know now that I can

trust my heart to guide me on my path to serve
humanity as we continue to take each step on our
healing journey.

Kim's story is a beautiful example of what is possible if we lean
into change and trust our heart to guide us with each step. I
have learned to embrace change and trust my heart to lead and
I have experienced many miracles as a result of walking with
deep trust and blind faith. It is not always easy to follow our
heart, especially when we are being guided to make some big
changes in our life. It requires courage. It may not feel easy to
embrace change at first, but once we begin to heal our fear of
change and shift our perspective around it, the adventures and
miracles we experience make it worthwhile.

The Healing Power of Our Inner Light

I am honoured to introduce you to Rosemary Laurel Messmer and her story about discovering her inner light. As we open up to explore how we can use words and sounds as tools to heal, a powerful inner light within each of us carries us through all the fear and doubts programmed in our mind.

Rosemary's Story

Many years ago I was told a story that has stayed with me and become a beacon guiding me on my path of healing.

The story began with the idea that we are each born with a light bulb shining inside us. It is a brilliant, vibrant, beautiful, and soulful light. As we go through life, we accumulate dust, fingerprints, mud, and muck on the light bulb.

The accumulations of muck starts to cover it up, and make it seem dimmer. This muck includes all the stories we go through in life that involve loss, trauma, hurt, shame, disappointment, betrayal, and fear.

As we start to believe these stories, we form the opinion that we are lacking as a person, that we are not good enough. We can't see our light anymore and we believe that it is no longer there. But under all the mud and gunk, our light bulb is as vibrant as ever. This light inside us never changes.

The accumulated muck causes us to think we have lost our connection to our inner light, and we feel disconnected from our true self. When we remember that our light is still there, shining as brilliantly as always, we can connect back to the truth of who we are. In the process of doing the work we need to do in order to clear the debris covering our light bulb, we form a stronger and stronger connection to our light.

This light bulb story resonated with me because although I believed the light was there within me, I couldn't feel it. I believed my inner light represented my inherent worthiness, but I couldn't find it. I couldn't connect to it. All I knew was that I felt a tremendous sense that something was missing.

On the surface, I was happy and positive, but

on the inside, I didn't feel worthy. There was a deep part of me that felt as though I didn't deserve to take up space in this world. I felt like I was a failure. I was not good enough. And I believed that I was always messing things up.

My childhood left me with a lot of mud and muck covering my light. I was anxious, co-dependent, and a people-pleaser. I was fearful of rejection and abandonment, because I had abandoned myself in order to survive. In order to feel like I could be lovable, I felt I had to turn off my innate joy and stop listening to my own inner guidance. Instead, I learned to conform to the expectations and requirements of my parents, caregivers, teachers, and the world in general. I didn't feel like it was okay to be me.

The feeling that something was fundamentally missing within me really stayed for a long time. As an adult, I seemed to be successful, intelligent, and kind. I learned to hide my inner world from others. Most people would never guess how harsh my inner critical voice was. I honestly didn't even realize it myself at the time. I thought the way I felt was just normal.

After I had my children, my marriage became the catalyst to embark on my healing journey. The way my husband interacted with me changed. It was so confusing because the way he was treating me didn't feel okay, and I felt triggered by this, while at the same time I thought it was my own fault. His tactics plus my own inner programming that I was not good enough created a powerful trap that kept me down for several years.

Looking back, I see my experience with my former husband was a gift that showed me all my hidden wounds. I believe we tend to attract life partners who will eventually recreate our unhealed wounds from childhood in order to give us a chance to heal them.

My marriage provided the triggers that revealed my unhealed trauma. At one point my own inner pain within my marriage got so intense that I knew I needed to figure out a way to change things. At first I tried to change my husband, thinking that would solve everything. When that didn't work, I realized I needed to heal myself, so I turned my focus inward.

I found a program designed to teach moms how to deal with stress, using a type of energy healing. I started there. Part of me felt like I should start with something about self-love but that felt too huge to tackle. I knew I tended to be stressed and anxious, so gaining some tools to be calmer felt like a great starting point.

As I learned to tune into myself, I felt a path for healing open up for me. It reminded me of the story of the light bulb within. I felt a renewed sense of hope, willingness, and commitment to look within and heal all the ways I was blocking my light.

After that initial program ignited something with me, I continued to find podcasts, books, videos, and other programs that were related to energy healing and intuition. I joined a yearlong mentoring program to connect to my own intuition and to clear all the stories I had accumulated that were blocking my ability to see my own light.

I started to find my way home to myself. I learned how to love and embrace all parts of myself, including my light. I felt less of a need to control things and I became less reactive. As I continued to do the work, I became more peaceful, calm, and trusting. Life became easier to manage and I am now able to navigate life's challenges with more grace.

There is still more mud and muck to work through, and there are times when my inner critical voice still shows up strongly. But I feel stronger in myself now. More capable. More connected. I can hold space for myself, and feel compassion and forgiveness for myself. I've got this. I'm here for me and I feel so solid.

By continuing to do the work to clear my own mud and muck, I have become more intuitive. I can now hold and shine more of my own light and have a greater impact through being fully present with others. The more I shine my light, the more of a healing presence I become.

As a counsellor, I have always had the gift of bringing calmness, compassion, and non-judgment to my sessions. When I set an intention to embody even more of my healing presence while supporting my clients, I witness a shift within them as they come to remember that they have their own inner light.

They feel empowered as they create a relationship with their true inner self, the version of self that is built on love, self-compassion, and a willingness to face their fears and to feel their emotions. They feel a deeper sense of peace within as they come home to their true authentic self.

I feel that I am living my soul purpose being an intuitive counsellor, being a healing presence, and consistently doing my own inner work. It takes deep courage and trust to live life this way (and a strong support system!) and yet it is the most rewarding, joyful, and satisfying way I can imagine living in this world.

Rosemary's journey to uncover her inner light can be a source of inspiration to many of us who were taught to be afraid to shine brightly and be a full expression of our true authentic self.

It takes courage, willingness, and sheer determination, and Rosemary's ability to embody these qualities is palpable and inspiring as she does whatever is necessary to uncover her inner light and answer the call to let her light shine.

Fear of judgment is a chronic illness that buries our creativity and self-expression under a huge mudslide of collective fear. I used to hide my light and keep my intuitive gifts well buried because I was terrified to share them with the world. Not only did I fear judgment, but I also tried to numb them out because I thought I was cursed or being punished by feeling so much of the world's emotional and physical pain. I realized it took a lot more energy to deny my gifts and hide my light than it did to finally let it shine. Building up the courage to shine my light wasn't easy but it was worth it.

May Rosemary's journey inspire and empower you to turn up your own inner light and embrace your authentic self more than ever before. The world needs you to shine brightly.

The Healing Power of Unconditional Love

I am honoured to introduce you to Yolanda Sarmiento. When I first met Yolanda, I felt like I was being wrapped in a beautiful blanket of love. Her eyes sparkled with love and she exuded a kind and gentle nature. Yolanda reminded me of my grandmother's unconditional love and it felt nurturing and nourishing to my heart and soul just to be in her presence. Yolanda's story can help shine light on the healing power of unconditional love and the impact that can have on others as well as on our own heart and mind.

Yolanda's Story

When I got married , I was twenty-two-years-old. I felt I was very young and immature. Looking back, I really wasn't ready to take such a big responsibility onto my shoulders. Soon after I was married, I got pregnant and there I was having a baby.

This beautiful baby whom I loved so much triggered many fears and insecurities in me. I was so afraid she would get hurt or sick, I was in constant state of alert. Out of fear, I tried to do everything in my power to control her environment.

I asked people their opinions about everything and I ignored my own intuition. I was disconnected from myself and, at that stage in my life, I was a very unconscious being.

It was only later on in my life that something happened—it hit me really hard and brought me to my knees. It was then I knew I had to work on myself. I started to reflect on my life and identify what areas of myself I needed to work on. I was determined to use my life experiences to encounter myself again, and I was determined to put the time and effort into making that happen.

I felt very lost so I asked the universe for help. Soon enough, the resources, people, the space, books, workshops all started arriving. Opportunities for my healing were put in place for my awakening.

One thing I knew I needed to work on was to learn to trust my intuition and to follow my own guidance. I needed to start developing my relationship with my Higher Self and to go within, instead of going outside myself for answers. I needed to learn that I have all the answers within me and that life is working for me, not against me.

After a few years of this process of inner discovery, I started having a desire to take a year off from work and travel. It was meant to be a year of travelling with my powerful Higher Self, while continuing to develop trust in my guidance and intuition. The feeling was so strong that I couldn't deny it. Of course, my ego showed up few times and made me doubt that this idea was possible, but the feeling kept growing, so I decided to give it a try. I was willing to accept any outcome.

I decided to open my heart and approach my work to share my situation and my big desire. When I asked for a one-year sabbatical from work, I felt my inner guidance was talking me through it and I was able to communicate what needed to be heard. The person who helped me that day understood perfectly what I needed and why. She gave me the biggest support and encouraged me to follow my dream.

After this request was granted, all the opportunities started to open up from everywhere, just like before. Pretty soon, my year off started filling up with opportunities for volunteer experiences, living in an ecovillage and, of course, travelling through various adventures.

Throughout the journey, I held my initial intention to develop trust in my inner voice; thus every moment became an opportunity to learn and practise strengthening that muscle. It was an amazing experience and a healing time for me in so many ways. I couldn't have planned it better myself. Everything came to me so easily and effortlessly.

I came out of this experience feeling stronger, more confident, connected, and trusting in my relationship with my Higher Self. I developed a deeper understanding of how to follow guidance. I was filled with a tremendous sense of gratitude in my heart.

After all the work I have done within myself, I know I have more capacity to show up as an even better version of myself. I know myself better. I feel more centred and more conscious of my state of mind. I am more aware of my feelings. When situations come up, I now have proactive tools that I can put into practice when needed. I know when I need to take my space to reflect or to recharge myself.

When my daughter announced she was pregnant, I remembered how it felt to experience the profound impact of my grandparents' love for me. I set an intention that I was going to show up for my grandkids in a way that would have the greatest and best impact. When my daughter delivered her first child, I was able to be with her through the whole process, from the beginning to the end, helping to deliver the baby, along with her grandpa and the help of the doctor. We each played our parts that day. I was able to be a healing presence, making sure she felt supported and loved in every moment.

Today I have two adorable grandchildren: a boy who is four years old and a girl who is two years old. My relationship with my daughter is close. It is very clear that my daughter wants me to be part of her kids' lives as well. I agree with the saying that "It takes a village to raise a child." I imagine a village where everyone shows up as a loving presence for each other. Imagine a village where everyone feels accepted and loved fully.

I have a deep desire to make sure my grandchildren know how much I love them. I am able to create a close relationship with them, so they know, through my actions and words, how important they are and that they are perfectly loved by me.

I show up in my grandkids' lives in every way I can: with decisions around daycare and preschool, for their birthdays, gymnastics, football games, and piano classes. I have been with them in moments when they are feeling sick; we have gone on family trips; and we have sleepovers together.

It has not just been about showing up: it is about the intention I hold when I show up. I show up as playful, fun, and loving as I can be. We have developed a beautiful relationship where I know my grandkids feel safe and they love to be with me.

Even in the face of difficult moments, my daughter and her family know they can count on me to provide help and support. If I can ease some of the burden, I will do it.

Through my work in the school system as a Special Education Teacher, I have introduced a program to the kids in my class about mindfulness and social-emotional intelligence. Also, I created a sensory room where they can have a quiet space just to be. I can see the benefit this has provided to the classroom's kids, and I want to transfer these skills to my grandkids.

I want to provide an environment that helps my grandkids cultivate the best versions of themselves by supporting positive development from the inside out. So, I am teaching them tools to live a happier and more fulfilled life, and to navigate life's challenges in a proactive way.

I started teaching the oldest grandchild about mindfulness and some breathing techniques. Also my daughter and I are teaching them gratitude and we made a song that we sing before having our meals. As the children grow, I will continue to introduce them to more ideas and concepts.

We are not a big family altogether but one thing I want to make sure is that they know I am here for them, that they can count on me. I want to play my part the best way I can.

I hope that my presence in my grandkids' lives will be full of connections and many adventures. I hope that my showing up as love will help them realize that they are complete, whole people, right now, just as they are; that they are loved no matter what; that they can count on me to love them and be there when they need it.

What a beautiful journey of self-discovery. I love how Yolanda realized that she needed to go within to find the answers she was seeking. Even shifting from finding answers in our own head to finding answers in our heart is so freeing that it also removes all the obstacles created by our limited programming. All the adventures Yolanda experienced shifted her out of fear and into love. Her love for self grew along with her capacity to show up as love for others as well. Imagine if we all showed up as a symbol and reflection of unconditional love for family, friends, and maybe even people we don't know. Imagine how different the world would be if we were all being love in action. Yolanda's story and her loving presence inspire me to embody love even more deeply for myself and others.

The Healing Power of Surrender

I am honoured to introduce you to Katherine Labelle. Her story will inspire us to tap into our inner strength and courage in the face of adversity. Just when we think we can't handle everything on our plate, we find a place within us that can carry us through it all.

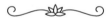

Katherine's Story

Until my late thirties, I envisioned and achieved my dreams rather fluidly. There were bumps along the way, but nothing of significance. Yet everything shifted when I followed my vision to have a child.

After a decade of trying to conceive naturally, sadly, my dream never came to fruition. This outcome was painful and not what I predicted. It opened my eyes to life's uncertainties. It also opened the door to adoption for the first time.

Once I turned this corner, the adoption process moved swiftly, and one year later, a birth mom chose my husband and me to adopt her son. Our son arrived three weeks after this announcement. He was such an incredible miracle.

I was so ready for the moments of joy, fun, and laughter alongside the challenges that come with raising a child. Yet the contrary emotions also presented themselves. I entered what felt like eternal hardship. I felt trapped. Isolated. Alone!

Six months into my son's life, I witnessed the first moment of his intense challenges. I knew my life was about to change dramatically. In what felt like an instant, my role shifted from being a mother to becoming a 24/7 caretaker for a son with special needs. The familiar taste of freedom was about to disappear. My dreams were moving farther from my grasp. How could this be? I was confused, frightened, and overwhelmed.

During my son's first six years, I taught part-time, an outlet I was grateful for. Yet, my son's special needs increased and teaching became no longer possible. When I let it go, I also let go of a thirty-five-year inspiring career as a dance artist, choreographer, and teacher. Yet, something about letting go of teaching made me feel terribly cut off from my community, from contributing to society, and from growing through meaningful connections with others. This was painful.

For what seemed like an eternity, I entered a journey of hardship in which my son had limited control of his emotions—especially his anger, his fear, and his rage. He was unstoppable at times. I became his everything and I created a safe space for him to show up in all his vulnerability. Many of these moments were so complex, even difficult to comprehend. But I just kept moving forward with each moment, each crisis, each breakdown for my son. I kept holding him for who he is in all his beauty, all his radiance, and all his gifts, of which there are plenty.

During my son's elementary school years, I felt unspoken pressure from other parents that I was supposed "to fix my son" because there was something "wrong with him." He did not meet their expectations. He was cast aside and, in turn, so was I. I started to pull away from connecting with other parents and families, because I knew they had difficulty understanding my circumstances. I simply withdrew.

As time rolled along in my hidden world, the milestones my son was supposed to meet were not being met. He was not keeping up with his peers. He did not fit in. No one understood him. He started being bullied. He was sad. Along with his losses came waves of grief for me. The day-to-day uncertainties for both my son and me were unsettling. Often, I wondered whether he would keep going to school or whether he would give up altogether.

When my son reached his teen years, the enormous uncertainty of his future started gnawing at me more than the day-to-day ones. Will he ever be able to live independently? Will he be safe and healthy? Will he have friends? Will he have a job? Ultimately, what will happen to my son when I am gone? This vast unknown is beyond comprehension.

Yet, I continued pressing forward as a staunch advocate, searching for resources and support. The job felt mammoth, never-ending. Burnout became my way of life. Yet, I braved the storm, endlessly advocating for my son to feel safe, to belong.

Looking back around the eighth year as a caretaker for my son, my sensitivity to feeling isolated peaked. More than ever, the human need for belonging stood out powerfully yet sorrowfully. Inside this realization, I felt profoundly disconnected from my soul, my spirit. To hold steady for my son, I knew I needed to feed my soul. I turned to spirituality.

First I studied Reiki. Practising on others

brought me peace and connection. I was reminded of my healing presence and my healing gifts. Reiki became the first in a string of three shifts that brought me back to my spirituality and gave me a deeper sense of belonging and purpose in my life.

The second shift was encountering Conscious Dance, a spiritual form that took me on "The Path to Awakening Love." Third and more recently, I joined "Heart Led Living" with Sue Dumais. This has been an incredible shift in my spiritual growth and learning.

Through the practice of Sue's work, I have surrendered more than ever to the hardships with my son. I notice I can no longer sustain this journey of aloneness, alone. More than ever, I realize I need to be in communion with others. I have aligned myself with parents and caretakers who raise special needs children. Their stories have lightened the burden of aloneness in me. I have reconnected with old friends from whom I had lost touch. Besides being uplifting, this gives me a much-needed break from my son.

More significantly, I have carved a deeper connection with my intuition, that felt sense of knowing what to do without questioning it. I realize I had become quite disassociated from my intuition amidst all the chaos. My spiritual work has guided me back home. Home to my intuition. I am so grateful for this shift.

In moments when I am intuitively connected, especially during times of distress with my son, I am better able to hold him in a container of love versus one of fear and overwhelm. This is when I witness him entering greater flow and ease. I see my son making shifts that are melting my heart. Shifts that I thought would never be tangible. I am learning to show up with a greater healing presence for my son and this is when he and I are most deeply connected.

The key learning here is that, if I let my mind run the show, I will smother my gut sense and in turn my rich and unique strengths. My healing gifts. But when I move beyond the mind and connect at a gut level, I can see that nothing is broken in my son, in my life, or in me. There is nothing to fix. Everything is happening as it should. The more I surrender to this Truth and the unknown ahead, the easier it becomes to open to intuitive guidance. And my true path awaits me and will unfold in its own Divine timing.

Embodying a deep presence and unification with and for myself is another key learning. This in turn creates the possibility for a deep presence and unification with and for my son. What I establish in spiritual communion with myself radiates to my son, to others, and beyond. I'm only beginning to grasp the profound possibilities of the latter, and to understand that healing is available to me through my own healing presence. It has a ripple effect on those both close and far from my circle and way out into the Universe and beyond.

As my intuitive acuity improves, I am learning to connect with my heart, the place in my body where my love grows and my intuition flows. And I am beginning to source the miracles that await me as I follow my heart's intuition.

This has not been an overnight practice but one of commitment, endurance, and deep surrender. Yet the more I hold steady on this path, the more the process teaches me about healing and how to heal. The more I come into greater alignment. And the feeling of aloneness eases.

I am learning that incremental steps are essential for lasting change and transformation. I am learning to respond versus react. I am learning to lighten common words in my vocabulary, the ones that could keep me stuck. For instance, when I replace the word "hard" with "challenging," the density lifts. I am learning to let go of the story that feeds my fears and overwhelms me.

When I allow my burdens to lift, I can enter and sustain presence. Alongside these healing strategies is the need for self-care. It too is integral to my healing, my self-nurturing. And even when I am unable to sustain self-care to the extent I hope for, I am learning to check in with my intuition and ask what it points me to right now, no matter how simple. This might mean stretching for twenty seconds, having a cup of tea in silence, or going for a walk. The more I follow my intuition's lead, the more energy, light, and healing resonate within.

I am gaining strength through spiritual practice and following my intuition. This helps me sustain my journey alongside my son, a journey that has altered my life. One that has taught me things I never would have learned about myself, about hardships, and the challenging position faced by special needs persons and their mothers, fathers, caretakers and, often, their teachers.

Even though I am still in the thick of this journey, I know there is an awakening ahead that I am open and ready to receive. I know it will come in its own Divine timing. I have learned to surrender to this truth, to follow the current of my journey as it unfolds moment to moment, and to notice the many miracles along the way. Every miracle I celebrate grows the gratitude in my heart. My love and appreciation expand. These moments of gratitude bring on the power of "YES" inside me. The more I hold steady to my "YES," the more I hold steady for my son. And together we ebb and flow through life's uncertainties moment to moment, arm in arm, one step at a time.

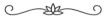

Many people think that surrender is about giving up, but for me it is about letting go of our limited human perspectives and fears so we can tap into the full capacity of our Divine nature to guide and lead us.

Katherine's willingness to persevere and approach adversity from a place of strength and courage is inspiring. Through the practice of surrender, Katherine taps into her ability to foster a deep connection to self and let her heart lead her through life's challenges. This is something we can all do. When we feel connected within our self, we can tap into a Divine wisdom that can guide us in every moment with every step.

I admire Katherine's ability to see her son's potential and gifts instead of focusing on his limitations. Her story beautifully illustrates how much the perspective we choose to hold will determine how we experience life. When we see life's challenges as opportunities to grow and foster deeper connections, we will feel empowered as we take each step. Life is our classroom for healing and for awakening to our full potential. Life is happening for us and every challenge on our path may stretch us, but everything we go through we can grow through.

The Healing Power of Unity

I am honoured to introduce you to Chela Hallenbeck. I admire Chela's courage to share her story. Many people are struggling to find their way in this wild world and I know they will resonate with her struggle and her sheer determination to overcome her fear and addictions.

Chela's Story

Healing for me means having the ability to move through the day with love, kindness, and compassion. Healing has been a process of finding my way back to myself, my true self. While I believe healing is available to everyone, it takes courage to take the first step and greater courage to keep moving forward.

For as long as I can remember, I have felt disconnected and alone, full of fear and pain.

My ego would trigger memories of myself as a frightened little girl who grew up in Laredo, Texas, wanting so much to be accepted and included and at the same time not wanting to be seen.

One of my sisters and I are biracial: our mother is Mexican American and our father was African American. Because of our skin colour, we were teased, ridiculed, and pretty much shunned on a daily basis. Even some members of our own family treated us differently.

I grew up with a real fighter in me. After enduring a lot of traumas, I was full of fear, anger, and rage. I have been treated for depression most of my life. I didn't have the ability to process my emotions in a healthy way, so I drank and used drugs to cope with life.

My ego would always go into defense mode, ready to fight or at least try to prove that it was bigger, stronger, and smarter than anyone else's ego. This always led to more anger and pain.

This negatively affected my sense of self-worth and my sense of security. In fact, I never identified with anyone nor felt a sense of belonging. My sister and I dealt with this in two entirely different ways. I became a fighter, a rebel. She basically grew up staying inside the house. She only went outside to go to school.

Not me, nothing was going to keep me from

the outdoors. I used to love going out early in the morning to walk barefoot on the dirt roads, climb my favourite trees, or wander off into wooded areas and creeks. To this day, I still love spending time in nature because it helps me feel connected.

My journey to unity and love was challenging because I had to see, feel, and heal an incredible amount of trauma. We moved to Dallas, Texas, when I was thirteen. Never in my life had I seen so many people with skin colour like mine or darker. I no longer felt so different; it was the best summer ever.

But that feeling was taken from me shortly after, when my nephew passed away. The circumstances leading up to his death are engraved in my mind, because I witnessed them. I was fractured that day. I literally felt myself leave my body. It was as if time stood still and a part of my soul remained permanently stuck there in that space and time.

The trauma I experienced as a result of his passing led to my substance abuse and my first suicide attempt. That attempt was to be the first of many. In fact, waking up in the ICU and hating the fact that I was still alive became the norm for me. I attempted suicide at least every two to three years, right up until 2015 when my healing journey began.

On top of witnessing the trauma of my nephew's

death, I also had to allow myself to grieve the murder of my best friend and the passing of more loved ones than I care to remember. I lost count after ten. During this time, I managed to avoid feeling and processing most of the grief because of all the alcohol and drugs I put into my body. The unprocessed grief and trauma turned into hate, anger, and rage. In fact, there was little else I could feel. I felt disconnected from everyone and everything. I wanted nothing to do with anyone. I wanted nothing to do with life.

Before I discovered and embarked on my own healing path, I really struggled to make sense of life. When I began to heal, I started to see myself in others and to see others in me.

One of the first things I learned when I began to heal was how powerful the mind is. About three months into my sobriety, the walls I built around my heart came tumbling down. I began to feel love. I felt an intense love for everyone and everything. I felt like an innocent child in a woman's body. My judgments had been suspended and I found myself standing in an experience of unity with all. I was in complete awe. The vibration in my body shot through the roof. My thoughts and words began manifesting so quickly that it literally scared me into complete silence. I was afraid to think or speak.

I had years of trauma, fear, anger, and rage

locked up in my head and what began to manifest before my very eyes can only be described as hell on earth. What was worse is that I was creating it for myself because I was so afraid to face my own trauma.

At some point, I became aware of the energy around me that was attempting to hold me down in this density of fear and confusion. At the same time, there was an energy of love and light persuading me to keep moving forward.

It wasn't until I became aware of how much my own mind and fears were contributing to the hell I was living in that I realized I needed to heal myself. I began to release feelings and beliefs of fear, shame, grief, guilt, judgment, condemnation, inferiority, superiority, and everything else that was holding me down in the dark.

What I have learned from all of this is that there is no hell and condemnation, unless I create it for myself. And that there is no saviour out there who can save me. I needed to make a choice to save myself. At the same time, I could feel a presence around me and I began to understand that when my heart is in the right place it seems to attract the attention of beings of light that are ready, willing, and oh so able to assist me. They are always ready to assist us when we choose to heal.

Healing for me has been about allowing myself

to heal all the layers of trauma I buried and, in the process, I have freed myself to unconditional love.

Healing myself has awakened and intensified my intuitive gifts. I still tend to hide them though, mostly because I don't fully understand them. At times, I seem to have no control over them. I discovered that my clairsentience gift allows me to say and do just the right thing to put someone at ease. On the other hand, it also leads me to say and do things that others consider strange. Sometimes my gifts scare me, especially when I forget they are not coming from me, but through me. Or are they? I really don't know. What I do know is that some days I find it impossible to differentiate between myself and others. It is as if I am both the creator and the created.

Then there are days when I seem to become one with all. The first time I experienced this I was three months sober. It was so alarming that it scared me right back to drinking. But only for a while because, being so fascinated by the experience, I wanted to feel it again and learn more about it. So I continued down that path and indeed experienced it again. I continue to experience it and other things today that I can't always find words to describe.

I believe we are all healers when we can hold steady in unconditional love for others as well as ourselves. I'm not speaking of a feeling of love; I mean love in action. It's about being kind, gentle, and compassionate. It's about being in a state of unity rather than of separation. When I am able to stand steady in love, I can easily sense the energy and vibration in others. This allows me to offer assistance when others are in need. Sometimes it involves something as simple as holding a door open for someone. At other times, just speaking a gentle word or smiling at someone causes a shift in both of us.

Some days, remaining silent and looking someone in the eyes causes tears to well up in mine. I'm not always sure if it's for me or them. I guess it really doesn't matter though. We truly are just one.

I can relate to many aspects of Chela's story and I love how it illustrates that being vulnerable is not a weakness, but a sign of incredible strength. I believe vulnerability and authenticity are qualities that can unite us no matter how different our lives appear to be on the outside.

Chela's journey to embrace her intuitive gifts is inspiring and reminds me of my own journey. Feeling different or as though we don't belong is not an easy path to navigate. I tried a long time to be "normal" only to discover that "normal" is not who we are meant to be.

We are all extraordinary beings who have a beautiful and essential role to play in the healing of the whole of humanity. We have been conditioned to judge others, which fosters feelings of disconnect and separation. We are conditioned to live out our lives feeling separated from others, and many people feel a deep wound of separation within their own heart as well. These wounds of separation are one of the leading causes of conflict, suffering, pain, violence, war, and division.

The truth is that we may think we are living these separate lives; yet we are way more connected than we realize. And the good news is that we can choose to foster unity and connection or we can continue to feed the fear and separation.

What if we choose to celebrate and honour our differences? What if in every moment of every day we made a conscious choice to feel more connected to others and to foster a deeper connection to self? The world would be a different place. We would shift into a world full of peace, connection, unity, celebration, compassion, and love.

The Healing Power of Self-Healing

I am honoured to introduce you to Kelli Taylor. I know many practitioners who are so busy educating, treating, and helping others that they neglect their own health. It is easy to get caught up in supporting others when someone is so passionate about empowering others. Kelli's story is a beautiful example of how we can use our own unique path of healing as a catalyst to empower others to heal as well.

Kelli's Story

I believe that one of the quickest ways to heal the planet is to start with healing ourselves. Beginning a journey to heal is a courageous choice; it requires both time and dedication. No two journeys are the same, and we each need to find what works best for us. For many people, there is some kind of catalyst that kick-starts the journey to heal.

When I was twenty years old, I was diagnosed with a rare heart condition. This set me on a long journey, which I thought was about healing my heart. Looking back, I can see that my heart condition was the catalyst to get me on my healing path. It inspired me to explore and try different alternative therapies and it ultimately led me to a career in helping to teach others the tools that have helped me.

One of the biggest surprises for me while working on healing myself was that everything and everyone around me began to change once I started to heal. A tremendous ripple effect happened just from the simple act of my self-healing.

Over the years, I have discovered new-to-me therapies and gained time-honoured tools that have become part of my daily routine, like breathwork, movement, meditation, and conscious eating. Each of these has profoundly impacted who I am and how I show up in the world.

Breathwork is a term used for various breathing techniques. I love doing this daily, especially at nighttime, to help relax my nervous system and quiet my mind for a better, more peaceful sleep. By breathing consciously, my mind slows down, allowing me to focus on the present moment.

One of my favourite techniques is "3-6 Breathing," where I breathe in to the count of three and out to the count of six. I keep my breath even and steady during my practice. It may sound very simple, but I have found the benefits to be huge. It stimulates the vagus nerve, sending a message to my mind and body to just relax.

I have also worked with a few trained breathwork facilitators over the years, which has helped me to delve deeper into my healing journey. The quick deep belly breathing was very therapeutic to release past traumas that were so stuck they were not allowing me to move forward in my life. I learned the power of using my breath to heal and be set free of emotional blockages.

Hatha Yoga has been my movement of choice for as long as I can remember. I started out as a young child being able to easily move in and out of the poses. But over the years, my love of Hatha Yoga has turned into a love of Yin Yoga and Restorative Yoga. These types of yoga intrigued me as they were slower, had a more calming effect, and left my body and mind feeling deeply nourished, rejuvenated, and healed.

This was the beginning of my lesson on balancing yin and yang; with the simple act of listening to my body, I could achieve great results. A busy lifestyle is considered yang energy and what I was craving was slowing down into more yin energy. Yin Yoga and Restorative Yoga have helped teach me how to slow down, check in, and connect with my body as well as to listen to what it is telling me. Living from a place where I honour my body is the single greatest gift I can give myself.

Meditation is something my mother taught me when I was very young. It wasn't something that I used as a daily practice until my twenties. When looking for a way to heal myself I came back to meditation to use for reducing stress. What I discovered from doing a daily practice of twenty minutes (or longer some days) was that this not only helped with my mental and emotional health but also it had a positive impact on my concentration and focus. I felt more settled in my body and could sense a state of peace I hadn't ever felt before. But the most important thing that meditation has given me is the ability to deal better with stress and to manage stressful situations more easily. Even today I notice that I feel off balance and my coping skills are not as good if I miss a meditation session.

Conscious eating is a relatively new term but something that I have been practising for quite a while now. It has helped my relationship with food by creating better and healthier habits. This practice in essence is designed to truly pay attention to all aspects of eating. This includes buying my food, knowing where my food comes from, preparing, serving, and consuming it.

Here are some of my favourite tools when it comes to conscious eating.

Making a shopping list: I rarely go shopping without a list. By sticking to my list, I avoid any impulse buying. My list is always filled with items from the produce section, which means I eat mostly organic fruits and vegetables. I also try to buy local foods as much as I can, to reduce my carbon footprint.

Slowing down to eat: I would say this is probably the most challenging habit to change. I can still find it difficult, at times, especially on my long workdays. Growing up with my family, we always ate at the table. But as an adult, I got into the very unhealthy habit of eating on the fly, eating while being distracted, and rushing to finish my meal because I hadn't made time to sit down properly to eat. The act of slowing down has actually helped my digestion and allowed me to be aware of when I am actually full so I don't overeat.

Chewing my food thoroughly: This was something I was guilty of not doing before because I was too busy trying to rush through a meal. What I have discovered is that by slowing down to eat and taking the time to chew my food properly, I can actually taste the flavours of my food and my digestion is much happier. To change this habit, I started out by counting how many times I chewed a mouthful of food, ensuring it was properly broken down before swallowing it. I also consciously practised putting down my utensils between bites of food. Eating mindfully allows my mealtime to be a peaceful experience and has made a positive effect on my health.

The years I have invested in my own healing have allowed me to be a healing presence in the lives of others. As I continue to grow and learn, I am able to pass on these tools and the knowledge I have gained. By teaching others how to practise and implement them into their lives, I continue the circle of healing throughout the world.

Kelli is not only a practitioner: she is also a teacher through and through. Her passion to empower others through sharing knowledge is palpable. I can relate to Kelli's deep desire to help others. I wholeheartedly agree that there is great potential when our own growth and our healing journey empower others. We can all learn so much from each other's experiences but it is essential that we do our own inner healing work first. Our willingness and courage to heal self can definitely inspire and empower others to heal as well.

The more we heal our self, the more we become a clear channel to hold space for others as they move through their own wounds and trauma. As we heal self, we contribute to the healing of the whole whether we realize it or not. At the same time, some of us have a specific role to play in supporting the healing journey for others. As we say yes to play the role we are meant to play in this world, we will empower self and can empower others. The journey to heal self begins by looking within. The rest of the steps on our journey will be revealed as we walk with deep trust and blind faith.

The Healing Power of Movement

I am honoured to introduce you to Miranda MacKelworth. Her courage and strength to share her story and overcome diversity are inspiring. I always find it curious which piece of the puzzle shows up on our path to be the catalyst to shake us up and wake us up. For Miranda, that catalyst was movement. Movement has always been a necessity for me. Moving my body keeps me feeling light and free and grounded at the same time. I discovered that when my body is in chaos, my mind is in chaos, so movement is an essential practice that keeps my mind and body clear and in alignment.

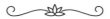

Miranda's Story

The dictionary definition of *alchemy* is one of "a seemingly magical process of transformation, creation, or combination." The literary interpretation is defined as "a process that is so effective that it seems like magic."

Emotional pain made me numb to my life and lulled me into a trancelike sleep. Eventually, physical pain shook me violently awake. On a journey akin to a game of lost and found, my re-awakening took me from frozen to flowing, and helped me rediscover clarity, strength, and healing through the alchemy of movement.

I grew up in a family that wasn't spiritual or religious, and I could not have explained what it meant to be healer. But I was always an intuitive child. I was curious and always asking questions.

Starting about age twelve and through my teens and onwards, I kept dream journals and read books on spirituality, meditation, and eastern philosophy. I always dreamed vividly, and later would often find myself in real-life situations that echoed those dreams, leaving me in a constant state of déjà vu.

In my twenties and thirties, I became a certified Reiki Master and Integrative Energy Healing Practitioner. As well, I studied Medical Intuition and countless other complementary healing modalities. I continued with yoga and meditation and developed a deep spiritual practice, allowing me to feel a sense of oneness and a connection to something mysterious and magical.

I felt confident and in sync. My intuition expanded and I received most of my guidance through prophetic dreams. I was able to help myself and others utilizing these skills, along with hands-on healing techniques.

I loved the world of spirituality and healing, and it always served me well.

Until it didn't.

Eventually, I separated myself from all the knowledge I had accumulated and all the experiences I had embodied. I sank into a depression and freefall. Although I had support around me, I had a feeling of complete isolation.

How did I let that happen?

As with so many things in life, it becomes clear only through the lens of retrospect. A series of family traumas and tragedies became the catalysts that caused me to begin to shut down. It wasn't the first one, nor the second, nor even the third blow. As my life continued to spiral out of control due to things I could not control—illness, death, and addiction of loved ones—I no longer wanted prophetic dreams or intuition. I didn't want visions of the future.

My dreams became dark and foreboding, and my intuition, which once brought me comfort and faith, turned into crippling anxiety and a sense of impending doom. Peering into the future to see events still to come became too frightening. Even though these challenging events were hijacking my life, the outcomes were very much out of my control. The only safe place seemed to be in the unknown.

Disconnecting myself from my intuitive abilities created a downward spiral that left me feeling unable to help myself, never mind help others. The impact of these stressful events left an imprint of trauma, putting me on a treadmill of fight or flight, only able to exist in survival mode. I don't remember shutting down my intuition consciously; it just kind of happened.

It was as if I lived in a sprawling castle and began closing a door each time I left a room, never going back. Until one day I realized I was living in just one small room, and I had closed off every other space. Even though all those beautiful rooms were right next door, or right down the hall, I didn't visit them. Not only were they unutilized, but I'd forgotten they were even there.

I stopped asking questions, at least the spiritual ones. I stopped being curious. I stopped laughing. I stopped asking for guidance, forgetting there was such a thing. Yet strangely, during that time— approximately five years—I didn't feel separated and I didn't long for connection. It was as though I was anesthetized, completely and utterly asleep.

I felt stress, fear, anxiety, and depression, but not once did I think of my previous accumulated knowledge. I knew I didn't feel good, but I couldn't even remember what I was missing. Was the shutdown self-preservation? Divine intervention? Apathy? Spiritual amnesia from the fight-or-flight response? Maybe all of these. Maybe none. But like going under anesthesia for surgery, I didn't even know I was asleep, or that I'd even drifted off, until I began to wake back up.

I started feeling twinges in my right shoulder. Having a very sedentary desk job, I was used to this and ignored it until things got so painful that I had little mobility left. I consulted my doctor and was diagnosed with frozen shoulder.

The diagnosis felt disheartening, with little in modern medicine to explain how or why frozen shoulder happens. The prognosis with a typical recovery timeline of about three years and no treatment options felt like yet another blow. The pain was out of control, yet with addiction to pain medication running in the family, I was as paralyzed by the fear of taking pain meds as I was by the pain itself.

I was in constant agony, even the smallest of movements caused severe pain that would bring me to tears. I had difficulty doing the most basic things—dressing myself, cooking, even holding light objects. I couldn't sleep, the pain was so great and I also had no range of motion or strength in my arm; I was unable to lift it or move in any direction.

I turned to modalities such as physiotherapy, osteopathy, massage therapy, and chiropractic for help. I had wonderful practitioners and they all helped in their own way, but no modality offered total relief. The frozen shoulder didn't abate and I was still in constant pain. As my arm mobility became less and less, my body tried to compensate and eventually I had problems with my back, ribs, shoulders, hips, and knees. I even struggled to walk.

A year before any issues with my shoulder, on a rainy New Year's Day, I was lounging on the couch. As if receiving a nudge from the universe, I came across a PBS special called Aging Backwards, featuring a specific kind of full-body movement called "Classical Stretch." I'm not sure why I tuned in or why I continued to watch, but by the end I remember saying out loud, "This is the key."

On a wave of excitement, I immediately ordered a DVD. Once it arrived by mail, I did the exercise program once before promptly stuffing the DVD in a drawer, where it sat untouched for a full calendar year. Whatever it was the key to, it would have to wait.

A full year later, in a moment of total

desperation, I felt led to go back to that DVD in the drawer, and I committed to this form of eccentric exercise (meaning it was both strengthening and stretching) that was aimed at liberating and lubricating damaged fascia and connective tissue.

It wasn't until the moment I began doing these specific exercises every day, working around the injury, and very slowly gaining mobility, range of motion, and eventually becoming pain free, that I realized the thawing of the frozen shoulder was the catalyst for thawing my frozen emotions, prompting my personal reawakening.

It started with a small voice that said, "Just say yes." I felt the veil part for just a brief moment, and I remembered a glimpse of how guidance feels. Oh, all those unoccupied rooms! I was terrified as I said yes. I wasn't even sure what I was saying yes to. I just stayed focused and held the intention to liberate my mind along with my body.

The words "Just ... Keep ... Moving" echoed in my ears.

As the gentle twisting and stretching of the muscles began to ease my physical pain and I gathered strength, the same began to happen to my mind. My creativity and curiosity returned, along with my intuition and my sense of being in the flow. The exercises deliberately and purposefully utilize all muscles and joints along with their connective tissue, and are deceptively simple, created for general heath as well as for people in chronic pain.

My story of becoming pain free using this technique isn't new. There are thousands like me, but I was equally transfixed and in awe of the creative, spiritual, and emotional freedom I regained. For me, it felt like the scene in the Wizard of Oz that goes from black and white to colour. How could I have forgotten all of this? The very magic and essence of life.

I've heard people speak of "awakening the inner healer." I had my awakening and initiation, and then I fell completely asleep. But I now know it's possible to "awaken the dormant healer."

I have explored many kinds of exercise over the years, from "the gym," to daily walks, Yoga, Pilates, aerobics, dance classes, and so on. They are all wonderful disciplines and they have worked in many ways, for others and at times for me, but my frozen emotions and frozen shoulder required something totally different, because it wasn't just about exercise.

I've heard the saying, "We store our issues in our tissues" and, through my experiences, I know that to be true. There is something magic and alchemical in this specific process of slow, rhythmic, gentle movement. As I stretch and strengthen my body, I stretch and strengthen my mind. As I move my limbs through space on different height planes, my intuition follows. As I rehydrate my connective tissue and eliminate the pain in my body, I do the same in my soul.

My blood flow improved, energy improved, and a joy-filled, pain-free life seemed possible again. I feel a new level of understanding of how a lack of hope can breed depression and anxiety. It can creep in like a slowly descending fog, gradually at first until you find yourself completely socked in with no beacon of light. The alchemy of movement gave me back my life, liberating me from pain, and reconnecting me with myself.

On reflection of my cocoon years, I still have some curiosity around why it happened, but I only have two choices: either to berate myself about why I let it happen when I "knew better" or to come to peace by seeing it as a protective decompression chamber where I slept in a kind of stasis until I was ready for the next unfolding.

Now, reawakened from that cocoon, the metaphoric butterfly, I have a different respect for pain, grief, depression, and anxiety. I hope my dark night of the soul can bring a sense of hope to others who find themselves in this process and feel lost in the dark.

I have struggled incredibly for quite some

time and I still have a way to go. I may not be the portrait of a healer in this moment, yet I feel that I still have a lot to give, and perhaps from a humbler and more vulnerable place, and certainly from a more understanding one.

The gift of reconnecting with Spirit, listening to guidance, and releasing the pain inside of me continue to be essential for my spiritual growth. In addition to cleaning house, emotionally and physically, the experience has also offered me a new perspective on compassion, empathy, and perseverance, and has renewed my commitment to being a healing presence in the world.

Perhaps even though I trained as a "healer" many years ago, it is because of this more recent journey that I can truly help others.

Physical pain used to shut me down because I spent so much of the first part of my life trying to numb the pain. I can relate to Miranda's story about finding a modality that helped unwind the physical body after a painful injury. For me, yoga therapy had a huge impact, because it would bridge healing in my mental, emotional, and physical bodies. More recently after experiencing a shoulder injury, I found osteopathy continues to help me unwind the deep fascia patterns in my body. As I continue to unwind my body, my mind continues to shift and open up more and more, allowing a more full expression of my intuitive gifts.

The words Miranda used—"awaken the dormant healer"— ring true deep in my heart and soul. I lived the first twenty years of my life as a dormant healer. I had so much fear of my gift that I kept it hidden and tried everything to try and numb it out or turn it off. I can only imagine how painful it would be for me to try and tune it out now that it has been fully awakened.

I feel a lot of empathy and compassion for Miranda and her story because I can relate to much of what she shared and because I had the honour to work with her before she shut down her intuitive healing gift. Miranda was one of the healers I met on my path who really inspired me to fully embrace the potential of my gift. She helped me dive deeper into feeling and trusting the energy as it flowed through me.

For years, I had no idea she was going through such trauma and had shut down her healing gift the way she did. I am grateful that she is finding her way back to awaken the dormant healer within. May her story empower others to wake up and fully embody their innate ability to heal self, as well as to say yes to unleash the full potential of the healer within each of us.

The Healing Power of Grounding

I am honoured to introduce you to Kimberley Maxwell. I am grateful for our connection and for being able to bear witness to her journey into motherhood. It wasn't an easy path for Kimberley and her husband, but through it all, she found a way to use her life classroom as an opportunity to heal deeply. There is a way to stay grounded in life's challenges or at least to find someone who can be a grounding presence for us when the ground beneath us is shaking.

Kimberley's Story

My journey to motherhood was a nine-year saga that brought me to my knees more than once. It was a process that broke my heart into a million pieces and then burst my heart wide open and made me a believer of miracles.

Sharing this part of my story makes me feel

vulnerable but I know writing about it is just another step to help me heal any leftover trauma from my fertility challenges.

Facing all the challenges on my journey to motherhood caused me to really look within, because the answers I was finding on the outside made everything feel more confusing. I got to a point where I couldn't trust my intuition anymore and I knew I had to do something different because the path I was on was causing me so much pain.

I changed my focus to heal myself, to mother myself, to nurture myself. Over the years I healed deeply and became a healer. As I learned to trust my inner knowing again, my intuition lead me toward the life of my dreams.

I started to trust my guidance even when it didn't make sense. I opened my heart and mind to the path that was meant for my husband and me.

This was a pivotal, magical, challenging, and transformational time in my life. All of the experiences helped me build a solid foundation of deep resilience, faith, and trust.

I remember having a vision when I was in my early twenties about adopting a child. Shortly after, I attended a spiritual retreat and I was guided into a deep meditation, where I met a little boy who would change my life forever, years before my son was actually born.

In the end, I didn't give birth to a child. Instead, I gave birth to myself and I was blessed with the brightest light in the world, my beautiful son, Tokelo.

The moment I saw his photo, I knew he was the boy I had met in my heart during that meditation and I knew that we were to become a family through adoption. I suppose you could say he was born in my heart. That is how it felt for me.

The sacred moment when we first met our son, Tokelo, in person is forever etched into my soul. I could sense that he wanted to cry, but he was holding it in. The first word that came to my mind was "brave."

My husband held him first and Tokelo bravely looked around the room. Before I took him into my arms, I grounded my energy and cleared my mind. I wanted to make sure I could be fully calm and present for him.

As I held him and looked deeply into his eyes for the first time, I felt the most intense love that I have ever known. I gave him permission to cry and he instantly burst into tears. Then he laid his head on my heart and fell into a deep sleep while I held him tightly. And with my next breath, I slipped into motherhood.

It was easy for me to cultivate calm within. After

years of spiritual teachings, yoga, and meditation and applying them to my life daily, I had learned to rely on a myriad of effective practices that consistently helped to bring me back to myself.

Looking back, I am grateful for the foundation of my daily practice of peace and calm because motherhood rocked me to the core. It was more challenging than I could have ever imagined. It has also been the most extraordinary experience of my life. I wouldn't change a thing.

I want to be clear. The challenges weren't about my son. He has actually been a really easy child to raise. The challenges were around my own attachment to who I was before I became a mother, and a whole bunch of other layers of my own leftovers that bubbled up to the surface.

As the months rolled by, the old me seemed to disappear and was replaced with someone who was confused, full of doubt, anxious, and frustrated. I felt scattered and overwhelmed. All of this was to be somewhat expected as a new mother, but it lingered. And then the mom guilt started to creep in.

It didn't make sense to me why I was feeling the way I was. I was a gifted healer, spiritual mentor, yoga instructor, and meditation teacher, for goodness' sake! How could this be happening? All of the work I had invested in myself over the past two decades was "supposed" to make me a "better" and more relaxed mother. It felt as though I became unravelled and lost in a very short period of time.

My son became a guiding light and a healing presence for me. He helped me to remember once again who I was. Who I am.

Tokelo is the brightest light I know. He embodies what it means to be a healing presence. He IS peace. He IS presence. He IS love, light, trust, and innocence.

He is the truest version of himself. He doesn't question his worth. It wouldn't even enter his mind. He reflects all that so many of us have forgotten: full embodiment and alignment with love.

He reminded me of all that I was at my core and what I desired to embody and model for him. In all the wild craziness of parenthood, I had forgotten that.

But how? I felt as though I was starting to fall apart, until one day I remembered the words, "When all else fails, go back to the basics." Breathe! Focus on the breath. And most importantly, I needed to ground and clear my energy.

To be a healing presence, I must be a grounded presence. I have a deep need for deep calm. When I'm scattered and overwhelmed, I'm susceptible to spiralling into those familiar wormholes of frustration, anxiety, and irritation. I simply do not function properly.

I recommitted to a daily meditation practice. I made time to consciously breathe. I created space to do other things that grounded my energy, like practising yoga, energy healing, exercising, going for walks, and spending time in nature by myself.

Everything shifted. I settled in. I was now able to navigate this new life and the new "me" with more grace and ease.

When I'm grounded, I am calm. I can hold steady in the chaos. When I am steady, my breath even, my mind calm, my body soft, and my heart open, I become unshakable. I align with my inner knowing and surrender to what is. This is what had got me through some of the most challenging times on my journey and it is what will continue to get me through all that life brings. Including parenting.

When I ground my energy my home feels calm and there is harmony. Everything and everyone in my family shifts. Things flow. There is peace. I am more patient. I sleep better. It enables me to stand in my authentic power, hold my light or, at the very least, get through the day without snapping at my child and husband. This is when I embody a deep healing presence.

Tokelo continues to help me evolve into the

next best version of myself, and by doing so I get to become a brighter guiding light for him. With every new layer that I heal, I become a better mother and our connection deepens.

In doing so we both shine brighter and I know that has a ripple effect out into the world. Together we are bringing healing to the world just by being us.

Kimberley's story is inspiring and reminds me again that everything we go through we can grow through and parenting is a powerful classroom for healing. Our mindset is key. If we set an intention to remain open and willing to heal, our life becomes a backdrop for creating awareness. We can find meaning as we face every obstacle on our path and unleash our inner strength and courage to keep going, no matter what challenges we encounter.

As you can see from Kimberley's story, if we can find a way to remain grounded and centred through all of life's challenges, we can find a strength that will carry us through anything. In times of struggle and uncertainty, when the ground is shaking beneath us, we can surround ourselves with others who can hold that grounding presence for us until we find our footing again. Grounding ourselves in love, peace, calm, and compassion allows us to be a healing presence for self and others in a way that it becomes a gift that keeps on giving.

The Healing Power of Faith

I am honoured to introduce you to Aparna Vermula. Her fertility journey has paved a path for her to practise walking with deep trust and blind faith. We don't always know where life will lead us but we can have faith that everything on our path is purposeful. Life has a way of directing us and ultimately all paths will lead us to our deepest heart's calling and to lessons that will support us along the way. No matter how many misdirected steps, detours, or distractions we take and follow, we will always be guided back to the path we are meant to be on so we can play the role we are meant to play in this world. Our heart's calling is always in the background, influencing our choices, consciously and unconsciously. It is a powerful energy that holds great potential to support our own healing as well as our ability to empower others to heal.

Aparna's Story

Building the tracks before the train.

With a strong desire to birth a child, my conception journey looked more than anything like hiking the steep slopes and building a train track with faith that a train would ride on it someday. In reality, it was opening the door to my own awakening.

I was fascinated by the story of Semmering, a region of the Alps between Austria and Italy, because it brought perspective to the thoughts swirling in my head. The story goes that train tracks were laid over this very steep and high mountainous section between Vienna and Venice even before there was any train in existence. They had faith that a train would come someday. Decades later, it became the main connecting line between the two cities with a stunningly scenic route as it passes through the mountains.

I embarked on my fertility journey with a plain longing to become a mother, assuming it would be an easy one just as it appeared to be for everyone else. Little did I understand that this journey would become the catalyst for me to step into my role as a healer.

I knew in my heart that I was on this planet to touch people's lives. But becoming a healer was not quite on my life's agenda. The healers I had previously encountered preached dogmatic ways of connecting with the Divine. The reprimand and negative feedback they used to course correct me, left me more wounded and traumatized than before. There was a distinct lack of compassion, empathy, and non-judgment when it came to supporting people who had had sorrowful and traumatic life experiences. I felt deep resistance to becoming one of those types of healers myself, but I also held the desire to be of service to the world.

Although I had had deep spiritual roots instilled in me since childhood, the environment I grew up in was dominated by a more rational, logical, and analytical mindset. I intently focused on my academic pursuits until one year a dear friend of mine had a sudden diagnosis of cancer and, shortly after, passed away.

Her sudden death shocked me, impacting me deeply; it moved me to pledge that I would heal the world and find a cure for cancer. This is where it felt like two worlds collided—my inner calling to help others heal and an academically correct direction to pursue.

After completing a master's degree, I interned at a renowned research institute under highly qualified biologists. It was a dream for many to be part of the research there. But there was a constant niggling in my heart, something I couldn't ignore. It felt as though I did not belong there. It was hard to understand what that was, but one thing I distinctly felt was that curing cancer was not my calling.

Experiments, paper submissions, and protocols aside, I was feeling into the energy of the place and it was overwhelming me. I was dragging my feet to work and feeling pretty much worn out every single day. I did not know if I would be permitted to quit, but the conflict in my heart was constant and tiring. Not seeing much of a solution, I sought Divine help and I pleaded for an understanding. My wedding came in as an answer to my prayers and soon after, I moved out of the country with my husband. The burden was lifted off my shoulders and I felt free.

My husband and I were excited to start a new life and also eager to build a family of our own, as though a dream was about to take birth. To our dismay, months passed and years went by, but nothing happened on the pregnancy front. Despite all tests coming back as normal, we were circling in despair. Life started to feel like a package of hope followed by impending sorrow all gently laid out in a monthly plan. Constantly having to look at our diets, habits, and love life under a microscope was distressing. Going down the medical route did offer some hope, but was soon lost in the miscarriages that followed. Heartbroken and numb with hurt, I became an empty shell of a person.

The years were now turning into a decade, still with no light at the end of the tunnel. I continued to put in my efforts, even though it seemed like an uphill task to get my husband on board and keep the flames of hope burning. The terrain of my heart felt raw and cracked open with pain. This longing to have a child was coming from a deep place, a tug at my heart that I could never explain. It wouldn't let go of me even if I wanted it to.

In this space of grieving, something strange and beautiful occurred. I woke up one morning feeling a bit woozy, as if I had spent the entire night with babies around me. It felt like a paradox. I was simultaneously sitting with the grief and disappointment of a miscarriage as well as opening into a sense of awe and curiosity.

I wondered whether I was imagining things, but I was also curious. These baby energies seemed to follow me around and I began to find comfort in their company. This awareness became a pivotal point on my conception journey.

Things seemed to change tracks after this

experience. I was drawn to practitioners who could truly hear me and understand my situation. I explored healing modalities that supported my body naturally as well as brought peace to my heart. Instead of coping, I was healing and it seemed as though I was finally laying down my train tracks, one piece after another. I was onto something, dancing around the edges of change, even if the change did not make any sense.

I began to see that my path to motherhood looked different from others and it was feeling more like a big jigsaw puzzle missing some pieces, in locations unknown to me. I started to feel like an adventurer on a mission to find those pieces. There was no map in hand except blind faith, and my body was serving as a compass.

Instead of constantly researching, I started to put forth any questions—fertility or otherwise—to my body. I turned inwards for the answers. The perspectives and pieces of wisdom my body replied with astounded me; I could have never found them elsewhere. It was as though my body knew the answer I was seeking.

I was happily following the breadcrumbs; my inner knowing was getting stronger and I was learning to hear messages through signs the universe would drop in at times.

At this point, I recognized that there was an

inherent sense of order present all along: the pieces were already there. I only had to see and accept them to embrace the journey.

This path became one of self-discovery. Slowly, I began to see purpose in my pain. It was healing me from within and I was expanding more than I ever had. I witnessed the pain patterns and traumas underlying my life experiences. The more I healed and released these patterns and behaviours, the more this created space within my body, mind, and spirit, and the greater was my clarity.

I was shifting old beliefs and opening myself to newer possibilities. At times, the healing would be so intense it would crack me open. Old layers would fall away and more expansion would ensue. I learned to hold myself through these changes with deep compassion and kindness.

I had the support of amazing mentors and a loving community of companions to fall back on without being judged. I could explore my emotional blind spots without fear of rebuke. My husband and I were still actively trying to conceive a baby, but I did not feel like a failure anymore. Instead, I loved the transformation that came about when I took the decision to get off the fertility hamster wheel of treatments, thus providing myself with an opportunity to heal, melt away the pain, and embrace the unknown. I saw that this journey was setting the stage for my own expansion.

The baby energies grew stronger every day and I was connecting more deeply now. Shut down earlier due to fear, my psychic space now felt as though I had taken the lid off. I felt comfortable receiving messages from the unseen realms. No longer held back by old limiting beliefs, I had greater clarity in discerning the voice of my inner critic and that of my heart when it came to following guidance.

During this time, I was noticing that friends and family would share experiences with me that would have felt painful for them to share elsewhere. I could hold a supportive space and even offer unbiased guidance, while still being non-judgmental and empathetic. They would go away feeling lighter and clearer about their next steps. I even found myself receiving messages from ancestors and spirit babies to be passed on to their loved ones who were serendipitously finding me through their friends.

The nudge to extend my services as an intuitive coach and a baby spirit medium grew stronger with time. I also explored my unique method of helping others heal through tools of Reiki, mediumship, and journaling.

Through this journey I learned to mother myself

before becoming the mother I was meant to be. I felt more peaceful with how things were falling into place. This helped me connect at a much deeper level with other women who were struggling to become pregnant. I could support and empathize with their grief as well as help them reconcile with the sense of loss they were experiencing. Opening my heart space to receive messages from spirit babies brought a sense of reassurance to my own journey and to the journeys of the other women I was connecting with.

The support I had received during my darkest moments was now rippling out through me to those who needed it. It was bringing the healing full circle.

The conception path became the bridge that connected me to the healer within. It was that tug at my heart I had experienced earlier and I finally understood why it wouldn't leave me even when I was ready to give up on the desire to have a child. It was in fact providing me with the opportunity to co-create this path to motherhood with the baby souls that were meant to join me, even before I was pregnant. I was receiving lessons to a more conscious route to conception.

This journey for me has turned out to be far more significant than just bringing a train to the laid tracks—it has been a sacred alchemy, a passage to my soul's calling.

Aparna's faith is a powerful driving force, keeping her living in alignment with her inner knowing that there is something bigger directing us in every moment. Her willingness to trust her heart to lead the way has the potential to inspire all of us to walk with deep trust and blind faith, and to trust life to guide and direct us as the life we are meant to be living unfolds.

Sometimes our mind gets in the way, trying to figure it all out. We get into our head, trying desperately to find the answers we seek. The mind is full of fear-based programming that limits our potential and narrows our vision of what is possible. When we shift out of our head we can lead with our heart and discover an unfiltered, limitless, and abundant source of guidance and possibilities. We can stretch the boundaries of our mind and open up to miracles that allow us to tap into a faith that will carry us through to new heights of experiences.

In the presence of faith, we can keep our minds open to the idea that if we are willing to be wildly open and deeply curious, anything is possible.

The Healing Power of Storytelling

I am honoured to introduce you to Julie Ann. When I embarked on the journey to write this book, I already knew that storytelling holds a deep and profound potential for healing for both the writer and the reader. I could have just told other people's stories in this book myself, but I really felt inspired to invite others to share their stories in their own way, with their own words. I invited those who felt aligned with being a healer or being a healing presence in the world, but I also wanted to include a diverse group of individuals to provide voices that represent a wide range of experiences so that every reader will resonate with at least one or more of the stories or perhaps aspects of every story.

Perhaps you will resonate with aspects of Julie's story.

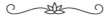

Julie's Story

I am a book publisher, writing coach and, apparently, I am a healer. This is the first time I have ever called myself a healer.

The truth is I never identified with that word before. That all changed after having a conversation with Sue Dumais about her idea for this book. When she said the words "We are ALL healers," something shifted in my mind. What a new idea! But it is so true!

I was inspired to reflect on the questions, *How do I heal?* and *How do I show up as a healing presence for others?*

As book publisher and writing coach, I inspire others to share their story and their wisdom from their life experiences. I have witnessed so much healing take place when people reflect on their lives and learn how to appreciate the experiences in their life journey.

I encourage them to reflect on how their life experiences and challenges can help other people. When they write about their journey from the perspective of how they dealt with trauma or how they have grown through their challenges to be a better person, it not only helps them heal but it also inspires and empowers others to heal as well.

I begin by asking, *How can sharing your own*

healing journey help other people? How can you be of service by sharing your journey with other people?

Once I have helped pull the story out of them, I then ask how they can tell the story in a way that will help the reader identify with them. *What lessons or wisdom can you teach the reader from your own mistakes or life challenges? What will the reader learn when they read your story? What do you hope will be the result of sharing your story? How can you help them to evade the same mistakes you made?*

By helping them to reflect on their own healing journey, they are helping others to heal, because the reader becomes inspired by their story.

I realized that I am the healers' healer, inspiring others to heal by sharing their story.

I think it is important to do this as a healer because so many people judge their own story as being unworthy or unimportant. They do not value the importance of their story and experiences or they are afraid that people will judge them harshly. I help them understand how their story can impact others. It can be difficult for an author to see this, and it takes a lot of courage to share their story, so I help them process and move through their fears and see just how powerful and supportive their story can be for others who read it.

I know how hard it can feel to be vulnerable

and share our life stories, but I also know how empowering it can feel and how far-reaching the impact can be.

In 2014, I stood on the TEDx stage and shared my story about being dyslexic. Through sharing my story, I have inspired others to heal their fear and insecurity about being dyslexic or having dyslexic children. I've changed their perception about this learning disorder and helped people see dyslexia as a gift. By being vulnerable and recognizing that judgment may exist, I've seen nothing but positive responses. Today almost a hundred thousand people have healed by listening to my TEDx talk. Despite my initial resistance to a fear of being judged as a "dyslexic book publisher," I realize I've healed many by sharing my story.

I only discovered later in life that I am dyslexic. I had to work very hard to have a successful book publishing company, and when I found out I was dyslexic, I assumed it would be better to hide this fact. It was actually a writer from Dyslexic Canada that I was helping to structure her story who recognized my big-picture thinking as a dyslexic trait. She asked me if I had anyone with dyslexia in my family. My immediate reaction was to say, "It would be very bad for business if I was a dyslexic book publisher!"

However, she changed my perception and I

could see how dyslexia was not a weakness and that many pioneers, including Albert Einstein, Steve Jobs, and Richard Branson, have used their gift as a tool for finding creative solutions.

I approached my family and it turns out that my dad could not even read or write when he married my mum. He was highly dyslexic and he had made my mum promise that she would not reveal this to anyone. This prompted me to take to the TEDx stage and bring awareness to the other side of dyslexia: that it is a gift for so many who understand their large right creative brain.

I know I have healed many who have listened to the talk and I know it has helped many first-time authors who judge their writing abilities as not good enough for sharing their story. I started an education program called InspireABook to help people understand that you do not have to be a good writer to share a good story. It is more important to share your story to help other people than to have good grammar or spelling. After all, as a book publisher, I have learned that you need a strong editing team to create a great book. It is the editor's job to turn a great story into great writing and, once my writers understand this, they are healed of their fear to write their story and share it.

There is nothing more healing than sharing your story to heal others.

I recently expanded my platform for healing by launching a co-creation retreat centre in Puerto Vallarta; it is called the House of Influence. The podcast show of the same name is where I interview people who share their stories of Influence and how they impact the world by sharing their wisdom and knowledge as Influencers. This is also healing the healers by inviting them to share their story in an interview. I do the same as I do as a book publisher by pulling out their story so they can inspire others to heal.

The House of Influence provides a high-vibrational environment where Influencers can gather to connect and collaborate on creating content across multiple platforms. The Influence of a book now goes way beyond the written word as a podcast, speech, audio book, video story, and documentary; it can also reach the creative platform of dance, poetry, music, and art. People receive stories on multiple platforms and this makes the reach for healing even wider with a greater impact.

Storytelling is a powerful tool for healing, because we all learn from each other's life experiences. If you have gone through a cancer journey for example, you have a longing to share with other people how you might have done things differently, or what you learned from the experience. For many, having the hindsight to read about someone else's lessons and then using that knowledge in your own healing journey is priceless.

Deep healing goes beyond a bandage to cover up a wound, or a pill to deaden the pain. It is a deep examination of our life so far, to learn from our lessons and constantly reassess our values and beliefs. The bookstores are flooded with self-help books because we want to learn how other people have done this quicker, faster, less painfully, and with a better understanding of the healing journey.

Sharing your story helps other people. You almost owe it to the world to share, so as to help one other person heal in a kinder, more loving and compassionate way. I am honoured that I can accelerate that process by helping storytellers to tell their story with more authenticity, vulnerability, and compassion. It turns out I have been a healer for over fifteen years and only today recognized it.

Julie has a gift in inspiring and helping others bring their story to life on the pages of a book. She helped me write my first vulnerable book in 2013; it is called *Heart Led Living: When Hard Work Becomes Heart Work*. I knew at the time I had to write my story around being born a healer, but it was terrifying because I was so afraid of being judged. Up until that time I had kept my gift as a healer secret and hidden. Even though I was afraid, I knew I had to do it. I lived much of my life feeling misunderstood and feeling as though I didn't belong or fit in, but I knew it was time to share my story. Julie was the mighty companion who encouraged me to write my story in a way that would allow me to heal as well as connect with the reader and inspire healing for them too. The process of writing that book was a deeply healing experience that freed my heart and soul to spread my wings and soar into the depth of work I am doing now. Telling my story was healing for me and for the thousands of people who have read my books.

The Healing Power of Miracles

I am honoured to introduce you to April Bellia. Her story is a beautiful example of what is possible when you choose to believe in miracles. I also choose to live my life as though everything is a miracle, following a quote by one of my favourite authors, Einstein: "There are only two ways to live your life. One is as though nothing is a miracle. The other is as though everything is a miracle." Even the challenges on my path are opportunities to heal, to learn, to grow. Choosing to embrace a miracle mindset opens us up to living a life full of meaning, potential, and possibility.

April's Story

I believe how we start the day sets the stage for how we experience our day.

Every morning I wake just before the sun rises and my first thought of the day is from an Ishaya meditation: "Thank you, Spirit, for my Life." As the sun begins to illuminate the sky, I lie in bed looking out my window and feeling gratitude for the sky, the mountains, and the city where I live. I think about how my day will look, what I will be doing, and who I will be seeing. I also wonder what amazing things will happen to me or who will I encounter. I create somewhat of a schedule yet I also allow time and space for serendipitous moments.

In my experience, miracles happen every day. Scientists have crunched the numbers of a person being born at a certain moment in time and, at that very special moment, all things considered, the odds are one in four hundred trillion. Think about this. Every waking moment is a unique moment that will never happen again. Basically, each one of us is a miracle.

I recently made a choice and gave myself permission to spend my waking moments living fully and completely. I want to create more miracles in my life. So I shifted my mindset and acted accordingly.

I had lived "by default" most of my life. I followed the script and checklist for becoming an adult. Finish school, travel a bit, find a partner, get married, buy a house, have kids, be a chauffeur, make school lunches daily, and so on and so on.

One day as I was doing the dishes, I asked

myself, "Is this all there is to my life? Because if it is, then I don't want it."

At that time, I would limit myself. I would keep my mouth shut, play small, tolerate people and situations, bite my tongue, and keep smiling through clenched teeth. I played out this role until one day I woke up from living on autopilot. I decided that I want to be the creator of my life. I want to be the pilot instead of the passenger.

This took a lot of courage.

The day I said yes to my freedom was a day I didn't make the choice. But rather, the choice was made for me. One small incident that started out the size of a mole hill had turned into a mountain and the circumstances forced me to reach deep within myself and finally speak my Truth. I had faced this mountain a few times in my life but I never took the leap. It wasn't time. I wasn't ready.

I found myself facing an intense situation where I could no longer make excuses or turn a blind eye. It was finally time to say yes to myself and face the truth that my marriage was coming to an end.

I knew if I didn't listen to this guidance, I would not be able to look in the mirror and feel true to myself. So I took the leap, jumped off the ledge, and suddenly realized I could fly.

While it was a challenging path to walk, it was

worth it. I freed my heart and soul to soar and I found myself dreaming again.

As a child, I learned how to speak French fluently and stopped practising when I got married. I used to love skiing until I had my first baby so I stopped skiing for fifteen years. It was a lifelong dream to go to Paris and I waited till my fortieth birthday. I was tired of hearing myself saying, " I wish ... " and waiting for "someday." I gave myself permission to enjoy and live my life now, not someday in the future.

I asked myself, "How can I create more miracles in my life?" I wanted my inner thoughts to match my words, actions, and experiences. Instead of just stopping and dreaming, I needed to take action and let my dreams take flight. I needed to say yes to experience more miracles.

I realized if I wanted to show up as a loving presence for others, I needed to start showing up as a loving presence for myself. I started to walk my talk, actually DOING and BEING an example of taking life by the reigns and living with a whole heart YES—fully and completely.

My life has completely changed and I am living the life of my dreams. I changed my mindset and the miracles are abundant.

The process of shifting my mindset from fear to love is how miracles are created every day.

Every day I practise gratitude, intention, curiosity, and finally, courage.

Today I am passionate about empowering others as an intuitive business coach.

I know how it feels to be standing at the edge of something, feeling paralyzed with fear. And I know how it feels to take that giant leap of faith and fly. So I help my clients, meeting them at their edge and encouraging them to gather the courage to jump. Sometimes I find myself pushing them off the edge, but they always thank me for doing that.

I can see their soul potential and so I act as an intuitive guide to support and encourage them to live their dreams fully and completely. It's a scary process because the majority of the world lives full of doubt, fear, and despair.

My wish is for others to embrace this one beautiful life with all the glory we are meant to experience. Don't wait for the miracle; be the miracle.

Life is full of opportunities to say yes to the experiences that will make our heart sing, our soul dance, and our spirit soar. As April shares in her story, we get so caught up in what we think life "should" be that we forget how to truly live and enjoy our life. We are so busy doing this thing called life that we go through it on autopilot. In the meantime, life passes us by and we lose sight of our purpose, joy, and happiness. Life is a precious, and each moment is a gift that is meant to be unwrapped with gratitude and in anticipation of the miracles and potential it holds. That is why we call it the "present."

May April's story inspire you to keep your mind and heart open to celebrate life and to expect miracles every single day.

The Healing Power of Rhythm and Dance

I am honoured to introduce you to Jacky A Yenga. When I first met Jacky she had such a grounded presence and I felt like a child again when we danced.

I have always been drawn to the rhythm of music and movement. I loved to play old records and to dance in my basement when no one was watching. As I moved my body, I felt a freedom and a connection to something that felt so much bigger than myself. In those moments, I felt free, grounded, and alive.

May Jacky's story inspire you to dance as you discover the music in your heart and soul.

Jacky's Story

Nkong is the *Maka'a* word for healer or shaman. *Maka'a* is the name of both my tribe and my mother tongue, from the East of Cameroon.

One day when I was a child, I heard my moms (my mom and my aunts) talk about how every single family always has a healer. It could skip a generation, but there was always an individual within each family who came into this life with the gift of healing. When I heard this, I immediately knew that in my family the healer was me.

Who that healer was in our family was never discussed, but I had that strong sense of knowing it was my role. How I was supposed to fulfill my destiny as a healer was a mystery to me since I was never told what was expected of me.

My mother is from the Maka'a tribe of the tropical rainforest. In my country, we forest people have a reputation of practising witchcraft. When people ask about my tribe, I always say that I am Maka'a, which is the tribe that celebrated and welcomed me into this world and gave me my foundation for life. My connection to my ancestors and the traditional teachings I received are from the Maka'a tribe.

My father was a Pongo man from the Douala tribe in Cameroon's coastal region. Apparently, after he moved to France ahead of us to prepare for our family's arrival, my father behaved in a way that caused my mom to break their engagement before she had a chance to move there. They never married, and she never left Cameroon, even though she contributed to a life in France that, in the end, would never be hers. I grew up in Cameroon until I was nine, being raised by my mom and her family.

In Cameroon, people would say that I am Douala, because that is the tribe of my father, and in many countries in Africa, the patriarchal lineage takes priority. Regardless of our relationship to our father's family or our cultural knowledge of it, traditionally we always belong to our father's tribe. The Doualas are water people. I have always chosen to honour the tribe and the land that received and raised me and gave me an experience of belonging.

At that time, I didn't know anything about my dad's family, except that he lived in Paris. I remember him as this mysterious figure from far away, which made me special at school and in my neighbourhood, because having a father in Paris at the time was unusual, especially in our modest circles.

There is a lot I could say to describe my experience of growing up in my country until I was nine, and my connection to the Spirit world. Like many people, I was born with a gift. It was never explained to me, and it was never nurtured. I guess I left my country too young to go through the proper traditional healing training, and then I had to quickly adopt the western ways.

My life in Cameroon shaped my understanding

of life and gave me a foundation for the rest of my life and influenced how I contribute today. It defined how I felt in and about life, my sense of being, my sense of my own existence, and my relationship to everything around me.

Growing up I was also aware of my connection to Spirit. It was very clear and direct. The way I experienced Spirit as a child was as a collective, like a council of elders in a village. They were there, watching over me, and I could easily communicate with them from within. Whenever something unwanted would happen to me, I would argue with them and be upset that they had let me down. I always assumed everyone had such connection and access to the same information.

My parents decided that my older brother and I would be sent to France to live with my father and his new wife and their two daughters—for the chance of a "better" life. Little did I know how much rejection and resentment I would face there, for just being alive.

Things changed when I arrived in France. The energy was so different! Mostly, it felt cold, but not because of the weather. I could no longer feel my connection to Spirit. But I thought I would be alright when I had learned the songs and the dances of the people of my new home. In my young mind, that was the way I would meet the ancestors of this land and be received by my new community.

I was shocked that it didn't happen. I came from a place where we believed that the dances belonged to the land and so did the people. Therefore, for me to be received in this new land, I had to be received in a circle of songs and dance.

Not long after I had been living in France, I was part of a conversation that completely shattered my beliefs about religion, spirituality, and the Spirit world. The people around me were mocking and criticizing those who believed in the existence of the Spirit world and the ability to connect to it. Apparently such beliefs were signs of a lack of intelligence and rational thinking, since the Spirit world clearly did not exist. I was shocked and profoundly confused. I felt that I had to adopt these new beliefs since, well, "white people knew better." But I also knew that what I had experienced as a child was real and my mind could not deny it, no matter how hard I tried.

I was torn and didn't know which direction to go. If I held my traditional beliefs, I might not be accepted in this new world that was now supposed to be my home. I could not risk that. At the same time, I could not deny my past experiences with the Spirit world. So, what was I to do? That moment created a split in me. I totally separated my African

Self and my Western Self, so that both personalities existed in their respective worlds, and I didn't have to decide who was right or wrong.

In France, I had to face harsh discrimination outside the home. One neighbour was particularly vicious and relentless in her daily racist attacks on me. Nobody said anything to stop her. It was as if she could sense I was the one without backup in that house. I was also facing mistreatment inside the home. Between daily verbal insults, humiliations, and savage beatings, I did not feel safe. I did not feel welcome. I had no one to turn to, no one to hold me when I was hurting. In fact, I cried myself to sleep every single night for months after moving there.

I had never lived in an environment so hostile toward me, and for no apparent reason. I didn't know what I had done and what I could do to make things better. I thought that God was punishing me for some reason. In addition to this, I had the intuitive ability to feel the pain and the darkness of the people around me. It was scary and overwhelming, and I did not know how to handle it.

Despite the daily abuse and humiliation at home, I still loved my parents, because I could see beyond their behaviour. That was my gift and my curse. One day, looking at my stepmother as she was yelling at me, I could see her whole life. I could read it all over her, and I could see it was not her fault that she was the way she was. So I kept forgiving her over and over, until I could no longer take it.

The year I turned twelve is the year everything changed. The abuse was relentless. Eventually I decided that my heart was betraying me and, therefore, could not be trusted since it kept loving and forgiving the people who were hurting me so much.

I was living in pain. I had the awareness of the contrast between my life in Cameroon, where I felt I belonged and I was deeply connected to Spirit, and my life in France where it seemed everything and everyone was hostile toward me. I really don't know how I would have survived all that if I hadn't had the foundation I received in Cameroon. It's not just about the nature of the experiences I had, it is about how I experienced them, and how it seemed there was no allowance for me to just be.

I was also living in sheer terror of being consumed by or stuck in the dark world of all the pain I was picking up around me. That is why I needed to put a shield in front of my heart. Eventually, I also blamed God for my fate, and I pushed away my spiritual abilities even further. I no longer wanted to collaborate with God or the

Council of Elders, until they either sent me back home where I belonged or restored my life in France into the "right" family.

In Cameroon I never had to defend what I knew to be true about the Spirit world. Everything around me supported my beliefs and my experience with the spiritual world. We went to church every Sunday morning and we also went to see traditional healers most afternoons. Whenever I would return home for the summer holidays after moving to France, my mom always made sure to take us to a shaman to perform rituals for our protection and make sure that our ancestors were with us.

The split within me grew. When I was in France, I was totally a Western child with rational thoughts and ideas, accepting Christianity and some of its teachings, even though I was not going to church. And when I was in Cameroon, my traditional spiritual beliefs were just normal and a part of who I was. Both personalities never had to argue about which beliefs were right or wrong—they each had their own world.

Things changed again when I arrived in Canada, and it is there that I fully allowed these two personalities to meet and coexist.

I returned home to Cameroon in the winter of 2001, a year after moving to Vancouver, and I found that my younger sister (on my mom's side) was sick. She had been anxiously waiting for me to arrive so I could lay my hands on her. It was then I realized that my last three trips had been the same. Each time, a sick family member was waiting for me to arrive and lay my hands on them. At the same time, no one in my family ever called me a healer. That was the year I decided to embrace my destiny as a healer, or at least to make room again for my gift, after years of pushing it away out of pain and anger. It was the beginning of my own healing journey.

My particular brand of healing has to do with rhythm, because if dance is the language of the Soul, then rhythm is the language of Spirit.

After I had an intense spiritual experience while living in London (I lived there for less than two years just before I moved to Vancouver), the healing power of rhythm became clear to me. My healing journey began with this premise: Rhythm is the language of Spirit, and the body is the doorway to healing. That is why rhythm became my primary vehicle to heal. How I was meant to contribute started to take shape, even though I was still trying to delay fully living what I sensed was my fate or destiny. I started by offering African Healing Dance Workshops for Women in Vancouver. Before each workshop I would sit down to meditate, and I would often have the intense experience of the joy of the Souls gathering at my workshop. The experience was beyond description. I do not see energy; I feel it.

When we sing and dance in community, we call each other back into presence and we move more easily into a state of harmony with Spirit.

Dancing is a state of being. Where I come from, our dances tell the story of who we are, and we dance as an act of peace, friendship, and trust, and to affirm our belonging to our community.

To dance together is to bless each other.

During my healing journey, I learned to deeply value and appreciate the wisdom of my ancestors and the meaningful contributions of my African heritage. My journey began with the intention to restore my dignity and, along the way, I learned that dignity, like respect, love, and kindness, is a choice. It is not something that others give you. You must first activate it from within.

I am still on that journey, as the process of healing is the one journey that never ends.

"Vancouver is not ready for what you have to offer." This is what a wise friend said to me many years ago. She was probably right then, but today, I think the world is ready.

Here in Vancouver, I had to grow to become the person I am meant to be. This is the place where I realized how I have experienced the extremes of connection and disconnection, and the sense of belonging and its absence, so I could help guide others. I provide cultural education as much as healing, thus fulfilling my destiny as a cultural bridge.

My hope is that we all keep blessing each other, and we learn to truly see or feel each other, so we can create a world that is truly caring toward everyone, and a world that we all want to live in.

My name is Jacky Arrah Yenga, and I am Nkong.

I have known Jacky for years and I have always felt a courageous presence exuding from her heart and soul. Although Jacky only shares glimpses of the depth of trauma and adversity she has faced in life, her abilities to persevere and use life's challenges to feed her courage and strength are palpable and inspiring.

I can really relate to feeling split and I admire how Jacky found a way to embrace both worlds she was raised in to become a cultural bridge. I love her ability to bring dance to foster community and authentic connection in our Western society.

The definition of rhythm Jacky shares sparked something in my heart and created an opening in my mind. It was as though my inner child had permission to dance again but not in the basement when no one else was watching. The saying "dance like no one is watching" feels like it changed to "dance like everyone is watching and you just don't care." I will continue to play with and explore this shift within me, but I know it will somehow free me to flow with the rhythm of life even more than ever before.

The Healing Power of Presence

I am honoured to introduce you to Kristen Bielecki. We have been so programmed to focus on what's next we miss out on what's happening now. Life is happening now. When we are present to what is we are present to the miracles that life offers in each moment. Our presence with others holds such an incredible healing potential but what about practising presence with self? May Kristen's story inspire us to discover what can happen when we turn our focus and awareness inward.

Kristen's Story

Being present requires awareness. It calls for awareness of ourself and our surroundings. When we are present, we can listen deeply within. Then we can act on what is heard and be a fluid channel through which the information can travel.

Deep listening takes the courage of surrender.

Surrendering into the moment of presence is to feel, to hear, and to connect with the truth.

The question to ask is "Am I willing?"

Am I willing to be present, to listen, to surrender?

It took me much effort and practice to learn how to be present, to listen to myself, and to surrender into the moment so I could be all here, with myself in all my feelings and thoughts.

As a young child, I felt conflicted because I never felt comfortable here on Earth and I didn't want to be here. At the same time, I felt there was greatness inside me and I was destined for something amazing.

This created a consistent underlying frustration, which led me to not truly feel like myself. I felt withdrawn, empty, and angry. I thought love wasn't available or at least I couldn't connect with it.

I really struggled to be present. If I was present then I would have to face and deal with my thoughts and feelings, and I wasn't ready for that.

When I was young, the feelings were often overwhelming as I looked around me trying to understand this reality. It made no sense to me. I sought refuge in nature.

I longed for love and comfort. Rather than receiving the love and comfort I longed for, I ended up being bullied in elementary school. The bullying went on for three years.

Due to my lack of self-connection, I didn't reach out for help or tell anyone. I became very judgmental of others and began to hate myself. I closed myself off from the world and, out of anger, I became a bully myself.

During the time of being bullied and bullying I could still feel this greatness inside me. And yet somehow I knew on a deeper level that I chose this life. I chose those circumstances to test myself at every turn to be true to myself and to open up to love. It took me a long time to finally open up to love and I learned many powerful lessons along the way.

When I went to high school, I was no longer bullied and I stopped bullying. I started to notice that other people seemed to know themselves. They were involved in activities, had friends, were stylish, and had fun. I admired this. I was inspired to figure out who I was. This was the beginning of my healing journey.

I spent time to reflect on my life. I had friends, played sports, and had fun but I still didn't feel like I knew myself.

So what did I think was missing for me that I thought I could see in others? This question opened my mind to discover who I was in relationship to myself, to others, to life, and to the world. I realized that I was just different from most others. I thought and felt differently. I was passionate and wanted things to be more just and balanced. This was what I had felt was off as a child.

The world felt so full of challenges that I wondered why they existed. I deeply felt sadness, illness, and an imbalance of life. At the time I couldn't put all that into words or make sense of it, so I continued to look outward for connection.

I tuned into myself to feel what sparked my interest and inspiration from my fellow high school classmates. The artists and intellects got my attention the most. They used their energy to bring something into the world. That intrigued me.

I befriended some of the women whom I admired the most. They were intelligent, musicians, lovers of life. We joined together and started environmental groups, educating others about healthy eating, veganism, corporate farming, deforestation, and more. This started my activism adventure to save the Earth!

Nature was always my sanctuary, so these activities awakened my love for life. The spark of life was ignited within and I started to really feel the greatness inside me. This created the knowing that I could know myself, love myself, and be myself.

One of the most powerful and effective tools I found through my journey is self-inquiry.

When I began to question myself, to understand more of who I was in high school, it allowed me to see that I could heal my hardships, pain, and suffering.

The more I could sense the possibility of healing, the more willing I became to inquire more. Self-inquiry taught me to be present and aware, and to listen and surrender within to heal.

It took a couple of decades to fully unravel all that I was holding to heal myself and to fully step into creating my life. The journey was deeply challenging but it was definitely worth learning how to fully know and love myself.

For me, healing is transformation—an alchemy through which we claim the energy we have been putting into an imbalanced version of ourselves that then gets transmuted with love into the full power of our unique beautiful self.

In my late teens and early twenties, I transformed my life by travelling, immersing myself in different cultures, ecologies, and lifestyles. This brought forth a deep knowing from within. I discovered that I had untapped wisdom on many levels, which allowed me to adapt to different situations, and to live in and love the diversity of life.

As I lived in the forest, defending old-growth

trees, and in my adventures overseas, I saw the same disharmony between people and nature that I had felt as a child. I wanted to fix it.

The untapped wisdom and energies in me began to awaken. I started to see a connection between our own inner disharmony and environmental imbalances.

I could see how our emotional and mental patterns created physical imbalance in the human body as well as in people's relationship to themselves and their surroundings.

I studied yoga, energy healing modalities, and herbalism to be a conduit of harmony for people and our natural connection to life.

I found that one cannot be healed or experience healing energy unless there is a deep willingness for change, for transformation.

With this realization, again I went inward.

I discovered that the most important thing I could do for anyone and for Earth was to be myself. So I meditated, did the self-inquiry, practised, and practised some more to understand and feel what it meant to be deeply present, to listen, and to surrender even more to know myself better than I ever had.

This practice deepened my willingness to go into all the spaces of myself, no matter how much it hurt to see certain aspects that I judged as wrong or bad. I sat with all the guilt, shame, fear, and hate to know myself so well that I could begin to heal and be who I truly am.

A stillness emerged that created a feeling of being centred and balanced. In this space it came to me that being myself means to be my Soul, the one who I came here to be.

This is what creates the balance within and without. I have found the secret that will balance relationships with ourselves and Earth.

I consider myself a facilitator of healing rather than a healer.

As a facilitator, I am present, aware of the information coming from within me and from others. The information shows me what needs attention.

I create a safe and loving container to guide people into their own self-inquiry to cultivate their own presence, awareness, and listening. I guide them into themselves so that healing can take place in full conscious surrender.

The way into the Soul is through being completely willing to see everything, to feel everything, and to love everything about ourself and others. This is the way that heals and transforms everything into the truth of who we are.

When I am with myself in the truth, my Soul speaks to me, because it is me.

As I listen, I gain the strength to be my true Self. Giving myself the honour of my presence is powerful. Being present with myself helps me listen and know what I truly need and want. I receive clarity around what is aligned for me; I move with it and make my decisions with it.

I choose to live from within.

I have become completely aware of my energy and the energy of others. In this awareness, love, compassion, and wisdom come alive in me. They show me when I am living my aligned life that it patterns reality into alignment as well.

Living in alignment shows me that it leads to being a natural healer with a healing presence.

People tell me it feels good to be around me, that I feel grounded and peaceful.

I can feel I am embodying the frequencies of purity and wholeness that radiate in the space around me, even when I don't have the conscious intention of creating healing.

The frequencies I am being automatically tune any space I am in, to what is true.

When I observe this, I notice it is easier for others to relax and be present around me even if they can't put a finger on why they feel that way.

The more I walk this path into awareness and being myself, I've found that in each moment there is always something to learn. And each breath, each heartbeat, each circumstance is to be honoured in love.

My journey has been about shifting from repression of self to full presence of Self so that my awareness has expanded to encompass the multidimensional field of existence.

Presence supports my capacity to be fully engaged with what I feel, what I think, and how I am aligned to connect with others and experiences.

In this engagement of life, I am able to connect with and see what others are feeling and why, who they are as a Soul, the causes of their challenges on any timeline, in any lifetime that I can perceive in the moment. I am able to lead them into the same powerful self-inquiry I do myself, to empower them in their healing and healing presence.

The purest gift we can give ourselves, and the world, is our devoted path into awareness and being ourselves.

Through working with others to guide them into their inner knowing as a healer, I've learned we need to establish patience and trust with ourselves. First, we need to open into the journey of being present, and surrendering to be able to breathe, centre, ground, feel, and to listen to give ourselves what we need.

This becomes incredibly life-affirming and builds a foundation of love that naturally leads to a connection with Soul, to Source, to the beauty, wisdom, and power of ourselves.

Standing on this foundation, I embrace challenges as they arise in life to get to know myself more and to gain the strength to master the art of presence, to heal, and be the healing presence I came here to be.

In these times the most valuable thing we need is ourselves, shining in our brilliance as our Soul and love.

I love the practice of deep presence through self-inquiry in Kristen's story. This can be a catalyst to remind us to keep going within instead of focusing so much on the outside. Each time we go within to heal, we contribute to the healing of the whole. We contribute to the healing of all of humanity, whether we realize it or not. Our inner environment will be reflected in our outer environment.

Our willingness to heal self is such a gift to extend to the world and it truly is a gift for you, for me, for all. I also resonated with Kristen's message to discover who we are at the deepest part of our Soul and to be our truest expression of Self in the world without apology. To shine as brightly as we possibly can so we can feel peace within our own heart and extend that peace out into the world. Practising presence with self and others holds profound potential to change minds, open hearts, and free our souls. Imagine how different the world would be if we accepted everyone unconditionally and actually encouraged each other be a full expression of Self. We would be living in a very different world. The potential to allow that new world to emerge fully begins with a choice within each of us, to be present, to be love, to be accepting, and to be encouraging to self and others.

The Healing Power of Connection

I am honoured to introduce you to Kevin Preston. Kevin is one of my soul brothers and fellow mighty companion in this life; I am grateful to walk beside him. He is not only a gifted practitioner but is also a gifted healer and powerful healing presence. He has an infectious passion for life that inspires so many people, including me. He is deeply connected to his inner spirit and fosters a beautiful connection to everyone he meets.

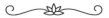

Kevin's Story

When I was a young boy, my grandmother would often say, "You've got such healing hands."

I was fortunate to grow up just down the road from the small farmhouse where my grandparents lived. I would find Grandma either in her big garden outside or baking peanut butter cookies inside. I felt happy and at ease around her, and saw she was always working away at something, so I would offer my hands to rub her back or her shoulders. She would then take a pause with a deep relaxing breath. She would turn and look at me with a smile and tell me how good it felt, and that I had a gift, or something of that nature. I suppose I did not really think much of it at the time, but when I look back, I can see that this was a common occurrence with others—and with animals at times as well.

I am grateful for an upbringing with three siblings in a rural farming community where I was easily able to access nature. A creek ran through our property; there were trees, pasture, little marsh areas, and so much room to explore and let our imaginations expand. It also seemed I spent a lot of time solo in nature where I had some tremendous experiences with wild animals. I learned later on that I was always sensing and feeling so much in my environment as well.

I had a number of powerful, close encounters with nature. I found myself nearly face-to-face with a moose in the dark one day, having stayed out in the bush too late. Another time I stood motionless for two hours one late fall afternoon with five majestic stags all within twenty feet of me, as leaves quietly fell all around us.

Of course, it was years before smartphones

and GoPros, otherwise I would have had some wonderful footage. What I did have, rather than photos, was a deepening sense of connection, and not just with nature and animals, but with myself. I was learning more about who I was. I was starting to become more curious about this growing awareness of being able to feel everything around me. I suppose this was a beautiful and natural time of development and learning. And then, over the years, I really went consciously further with so much more than just using my ears to listen.

I believe it was part of my connection with the natural world that eventually led me to study and become a doctor of Traditional Chinese Medicine. The ancient knowledge drew me in, along with its pure effectiveness and practicality.

I was always fascinated with wanting to understand how things worked, and how that could be applied to make things better. At school, I loved math and science. I grew to love biology even more, along with studying energy or what's known as "Qi." I began to feel where small convergences of energy would be accumulated or blocked along the meridian pathways of the body, and how acupuncture, a gentle touch, or even pure observation with loving intention could shift and restore flow once again. At times, almost instantly.

I have witnessed full body hives disappear

within minutes with properly done acupuncture, when even high dose antihistamines weren't working. I've seen fevers drop by several degrees, or incredibly intense anxiety attacks settle down, and the patient then falls into a restful sleep. It's been the greatest blessing to observe the innate healing capability of the human body supported by these ancient methods.

Time and time again, witnessing the body's ability to respond to various treatments continually fueled my motivation to see what further possibilities exist. To this day, that learning and desire has not stopped.

I am blessed to be following a path that leads me to question and understand the deeper function of all things, from the planet in the macrocosm, to the internal environments of my patients in the microcosm. All things are connected, especially when it comes to our biology. We cannot compartmentalize ourselves, or our illnesses and diseases in the way we thought we could. The vast interconnected web of life can be overlooked; so, if we choose to take the time to look deeper, patterns always begin to emerge.

Patterns in the realm of Chinese medicine are main hallmarks we are trained to discern when looking at the symptom picture of a patient. The symptoms themselves don't tell us the cause but, when we start looking from a higher perspective, we can often begin to see how they may have come to be. We can discover why the biology of the body is expressing itself in a certain way, with a particular set of patterns, and from there we can follow the flow down to the probable root causes.

I believe part of my role in medicine is to help patients see where areas of their lives are in flow and where they are not, and then to give tools, resources, and treatments to close that gap. The body desires harmony, so if we know the elements of how to bring that into the light then health can return. Health and balance are in our DNA. They are in our consciousness. More than that, they are in our love for life. Our love for each other's journey here as well as our own.

I have noticed that being in a loving internal state the best I can be, and being present, clear, and as a neutral soul witness are enough to create a healing cascade for myself and others.

We are our own medicine. What inspires me most is to help awaken the medicine and healing capability in others. Sparking or bringing forward their own potential within their biology, and then being able to witness incredible transformations. When a human being reconnects into their own authenticity again, they become so much more empowered, resourceful, and healthy.

The spirit, or "shen," in my patients' eyes might have become dim. The spirit returning into my patients' eyes is truly one of the loveliest things to see. The brightness and liveliness, the shining potential showing through. It can be felt. The presence of their energy returning and how that alters all of their interactions with friends and loved ones, and within their community.

It is a node of humanity lighting up that adds to the whole, and certainly a human being feeling genuine happiness and gratitude is a force to be reckoned with. From that vibration or frequency of living, the internal environment reshapes itself along with an improved function of the cells, and the communication network inside shimmers and crackles with clarity and purpose.

Vitality and enthusiasm for life; to me that is health.

Kevin's ability to connect deeply and authentically with others helps them see and feel the truth of who they are. He is like a mirror reflecting back all the beauty and potential that resides within them.

When we make a conscious choice to foster deeper, more authentic connections with self, with others, with nature, with life, we unleash a potential to remember our true essence is love. And love is powerful force for change, for healing, for transformation.

Can you feel a connection to the potential that love carries within you? It is ready to be unleashed.

The Healing Power of Perspective

I am honoured to introduce you to Surya Devi. I believe life has a way of directing and guiding us. At the same time we can be co-creators as we bridge our humanness and our Divinity, and let love animate us in every moment. The perspective we choose to hold can empower us.

Surya's Story

My healing journey started because I needed healing.

It didn't look that way on the outside. After becoming interested in various spiritual topics as a teenager, and upon returning from a trip to South America, I signed up to do a healing bodywork course to learn various styles of holistic massage. This began a journey of two decades and more of studying and practising the healing arts.

I signed up for a Reiki healing course at the same time and I vividly remember having some of my first experiences of deep peace while lying on the massage table receiving Reiki from the other students. The soft, soothing music the instructor played took me away to a space where, for the first time, I felt a sense of home.

Like many other people, I have always felt a bit out of place in the world. My deep sensitivity allowed me to pick up on the energy of others and I always had an inner knowing when something was off or not as it was being presented. The more I found out about what went on all over the planet, the more my heart ached for humanity.

My ego was excited for me to become a "healer" and, for many years, I was very attached to being the one in the position of helping others. I studied various kinds of energy-healing modalities and offered treatments to clients both paid and at public gatherings where other healers and I would offer sessions for free or for a donation.

It wasn't until over a decade into my journey that I had a rude awakening, or perhaps it was a humbling of sorts. I realized that, although I was able to serve and help others, I was also in need of deep personal healing myself. I needed to heal myself in order to truly access the frequency needed to embody pure, divine source energy.

After a series of devastating happenings that I lovingly call "seven years of hell," I realized I had much more work to do in clearing my own issues so as to be fully of service to others. Since then I have dedicated much of my life and practice to self-healing, which continues to this day.

The other day I had a thought: *Healers, are you still a healer even if you don't have a client or student? Will you still serve, even when there seemingly is no one to serve?*

Answering yes to these questions means that regardless of however another individual factors into a situation, we can still embody the energy of healing and do the work on ourselves, or as a prayer for the planet, the cosmos, and the galaxy.

This is what being a healing presence means to me: recognizing that every thought, word, and action we take here has a consequence, creates a ripple, and/or has an effect somewhere.

It is my current belief and understanding that perhaps the greatest service we can offer humanity is to truly BE the healing presence. When we embody the energy of divine light and radiate love from the heart centre, this immediately creates positive energy in the world.

When we practise this, we can take our love

everywhere we go. Healing energy is so powerful and profound that it can affect someone just from being in our vicinity. It can reverberate through our words when we speak and it can sparkle in our eyes as we smile at another.

Now I realize that, even if I never saw another client or taught another class again, I will always be a healer.

The energy of healing lives within me and it serves as a catalyst for anyone who comes into contact with me.

I believe you are a healing presence too. Open your heart and walk forward bravely, with trust, passion, and reverence for all of life.

We can all be a healing presence when we embody divine grace, and speak and live from the heart.

The conditioning of the world will have us lost inside of the mind, probably thinking fearful, limited thoughts and wondering whether we are good enough. When we begin the process of expanding our consciousness, we begin to see everything differently. We see there are infinite possibilities, we are worthy beyond measure, and we can choose to change the way we perceive things.

I used to think that one day I would reach some kind of enlightened space that would free me from my suffering and that my life would be perfect thanks to my newly acquired spiritual knowledge. However, in my experience, it has actually been something different. The more I learn and grow, the less I feel like I know—I continue to be in awe of life and all its complexities. There are almost always various problems and issues taking place in life; however, the benefit of walking the spiritual path is that we can gather tools that will help us navigate the more troubling times.

A few years ago I was set to go on the trip of a lifetime with my Tibetan teacher and a large group of students from Canada, America, China, and Taiwan. My teacher is from a remote village in the mountains of Tibet, so we all prepared to be roughing it on the mountain tops first. We arrived in China and spent a few days there before starting the journey to his village. At a government checkpoint in Tibet, authorities refused to let us go any further, even though we had all the correct paperwork and permissions to enter. We were all disappointed. We had been waiting to meet everyone in the village for a long time and it was meant to be a special meeting to receive a special empowerment and some other blessings.

Any attempts to dispute this were unsuccessful and, the next morning, we were chased out of that small town by police and ended up back in the city we had flown into. We were quite a large group and nowhere had space for all of us to stay, except for the top five star hotel. Luckily, there was a very wealthy man from Shanghai in our group; he offered to pay for us all to stay in the five star hotel. This is where our Tibetan teacher joined us and gave us the empowerment blessing. The trip changed altogether and we spent the rest of the time touring several mountainous regions in China.

One night at dinner, our teacher said to us, "I am so proud of all of you. Not one of you got angry or upset about us not being able to go to the village as planned. This is how I know the dharma (the teachings of the Buddha) are working. I am so proud."

This is the purpose of the spiritual path as I see it. Although the modern day message we may get from many healers and coaches is that being spiritual will give us the power to manifest everything that we desire, this is not exactly its purpose in my eyes.

Of course, it is wonderful to enjoy the good things in life and learn to flex our manifestation muscles. However, the real blessing is more like what happened on our trip to China. It is a wonderful achievement to not become angry, resentful, or blow up, which we might have once done. It is also wonderful to practise compassion for all beings and do our best to try to understand someone else before judging them. To be able to go with the flow—no matter what is happening—is also an incredible skill to practise and master.

I have always said that perhaps life isn't about getting what we want but being happy whether we get it or not. This is what the Buddhists would probably call non-attachment. It is the ability to detach and see things objectively, to stop reacting emotionally to everyone and everything. This is the real spiritual gold as I see it.

You may have heard the saying before that the present is the gift, and it is something to never forget. The magic is always in the present moment. The more we learn to be present, the more we can become a true healing presence for love wherever we go.

Surya's story is a beautiful journey of discovering the power of perspective and find out how we can make a conscious choice to see beauty and to trust the Divine orchestration of our lives in every moment. As life unfolds before our eyes, we can remind ourselves that we are only seeing a limited perspective through our human eyes and that we have the ability to tap into an inner level of trust and faith that brings us closer to reaching a perspective of our Divine sight. That means we are often walking with deep trust and blind faith, but the more we do that the more we trust life is happening for us, through us, and as us. That is the perspective I choose to hold and it is one that has freed my mind from fear. For that I am deeply grateful and eternally free.

The Healing Power of Love

I am honoured to introduce you to my soul sister and fellow mighty companion Reverend Lisa Windsor. We have walked through many of life's challenges together and have been a powerful healing presence for each other in many ways. Lisa is a true gift and miracle in my life and I know that feeling is mutual. I believe we were meant to meet when we did and be mighty companions for each other as we moved through the deepest, darkest, heaviest layers of healing so we could step into the light as messengers of love in this world fully, wholly, and completely. Lisa is the embodiment of joy and love in the world, and I am honoured to share her story and her healing presence in this book.

Reverend Lisa's Story

Earlier in my life, I would not have described myself as a healing presence. I would have said I had a worried or stressful presence covered over by the appearance of confidence and poise.

My healing journey began when I became increasingly aware of acute inner anxiety. Before that, I lived with high levels of inner pain, such as racing thoughts and daily stomachaches that I thought were normal. But slowly, I started to wake up to this pain. I started questioning. *Is it normal to feel sick to my stomach every day? Is it normal for my thoughts to be fearful, threatening, and incessant?*

As I became aware of my inner chaos, I started asking those around me whether they had similar inner experiences and every one of them said YES! Soon after, a trusted teacher told me that she had healed her own anxiety. It seemed unbelievable, yet I knew she was telling the truth. Right there and then, I vowed to heal myself.

Never did I imagine that the answer for healing would come in the form of a spiritual path called *A Course in Miracles* (ACIM). It is a pathway for undoing the thought system of fear and guilt in the mind (ego). It teaches systematically (through a daily workbook practice) to train the mind to align with love. In ACIM, God is perfect love and so the words God and love can be interchanged.

Healing was defined for me as undoing the blocks to love's (God's) presence. I had a lot of blocks! ACIM teaches that every judgment, grievance and attack thought we hold is a block to our peace of mind. It teaches a process of forgiveness that empowers us to release fear and open to the presence of love. A miracle is a shift in perception from fear to love.

I dedicated my life to studying and applying the principles of *A Course in Miracles.* My experiences and relationships were my classrooms for healing as they presented countless opportunities to practise forgiveness. For the last two decades, I have been focused on healing and, as a result, I have experienced an inner transformation.

As my mind healed, I could feel the presence of love (God) within me. This healing presence cannot be contained or limited, and so I have noticed that I became more loving, patient, and kind to those around me. I believe we are all meant to be a healing presence for the people in our lives.

When I became an Ordained Spiritual Minister, I was taught a new definition of *ministry,* which simply meant the act of sharing or extending God's Love. Just like everyone is a healing presence, I could say that we all have a ministry. It is our family, friends, community, workplace, pets, and so on.

When I am connected with this healing presence, the underlying messages that are communicated to those around me are these: *I see you, I hear you, I have time for you, you matter, you are innocent, and you are loved beyond measure.* When I am present with another, what feels most important is the connection, the listening, the non-judgment, and ultimately the presence of LOVE, which is the true healing agent. God is the healing agent.

I have been called to be a healing presence or minister in all facets of my life. As a mom, I am a healing presence for my kids. At times, I am called to be a healing presence for my friends and, consistently, I stand as a healing presence in my spiritual community, Modern Miracles.

Here are three powerful stories of times when I have been called into that presence of love and the miracles that have rippled out from those impactful moments.

I have four kids and when they were aged two, four, six, and eight, I was in the middle of a very painful divorce. I was racked with worry and fear that I was failing as a mom and that I could lose my kids to the favour of their dad. My now ex-husband had access to money and resources that I did not. We had shared parenting time with the kids, and whenever they were with him, he spent a lot of money buying them new things, eating out at restaurants, and doing fun activities. When the kids were home with me, things were simple and basic without any extras. I worried that the kids would be captivated by all the sparkle and glitter, and start to prefer being with their dad.

I prayed for help in changing my mind about this situation. An answer came that had a lasting impact. As I stood in my living room, I felt a light turn on inside of me. I felt my heart open and the light emulating outward and all around. I could feel the loving words of my inner teacher (Holy Spirit), impressing on my mind.

You are a lighthouse for your children. The light is always on and the door of your heart is always open. Free your kids to come and go from this place of love and safety. As you continue to stand steady in this light, your kids will know they have a safe loving place where they can always rest, where they can always return.

This taught me that I was meant to be a healing presence for my kids. I had to free them to walk their paths and I had to trust that they would feel and know my heart and love were always steady, ready to embrace them with compassion and understanding.

I have also learned to be truly helpful in my friendships. On one particular Valentine's Day, I had tentative plans to meet my friend Sarah for coffee. I had asked her for help with a project I was working on. The plans were tentative because she was holding out hope that she might have a date for Valentine's Day. I laughed and told her, I think I am your "date." Sure enough, we met up that afternoon and almost immediately she told me she wasn't really interested in helping out with my project. Interestingly, instead of getting triggered and upset, I felt a shift to curiosity because I knew we were meant to meet that day.

Sarah started opening up about the challenges she was facing in her life. I had no idea things had been so difficult for her. My inner teacher (Holy Spirit) communicated intuitively that part of my continued training as an ordained minister was to learn about the true meaning of ministry. *Your job is to love her. Tell her silently: I see you, I hear you, I'm so glad you are sharing all of this with me. I love you. You are not alone.*

I was called to be a healing presence in her life and, honestly, it was a huge gift for both of us. We could feel God's Love orchestrating the entire experience. I showed up to serve God's plan. Sarah would never have asked for help directly. She showed up because she thought she might be helping me when she was the one who really needed support. And I learned that I was called to be a healing presence and represent God's Love. I always think of her on Valentine's

Day as one of my favourite Valentine's dates ever.

As a spiritual minister, I am called daily to be a healing presence for my community. One day, I was preparing for a full-day workshop based on the spiritual teachings of *A Course in Miracles*. In the days leading up, I kept asking my inner teacher (Holy Spirit) for clarity about the theme of this workshop. Over twenty people had registered and I was starting to get nervous that I wouldn't be prepared. This has been a challenge for me because ACIM teaches that everything will be planned for me, and whatever I need to know will be shared with me at the perfect time. I turned within and asked my inner teacher (Holy Spirit) how I could see this differently.

I was shown that I always want to add "bells and whistles" to what I'm teaching because I have an underlying fear that it's not going to be enough. That I'm not enough. I heard the Holy Spirit whisper in my mind, *Your presence is enough. It's all that is required. Show up with presence, and all will flow with ease and grace.*

I showed up at the workshop and in the opening circle, I sat staring at the blank piece of paper in front of me. I sat silently, with an open mind, trusting that clarity would come. Staring at the blank piece of paper, I realized it was meant to represent the clear and present moment. This now moment was where we can hear God's voice. From that blank piece of paper, the Holy Spirit can write the words and I can speak them. And that is exactly what happened. The day unfolded with so many miracles. And I learned to simply be a healing presence; I learned that my presence is the most powerful gift I can give.

We are here to be a healing presence for those in our lives. It requires that we focus on our own healing first. Once we are healed, our healing presence is in us to share. It is not to be limited; it extends to our families, friends, co-workers, communities, the whole world.

Our healing presence silently communicates, I see you, I hear you, I have time for you, I love you.

We do not heal alone. There is an interlocking chain of miracles that unfolds as we take our rightful place in God's healing plan.

Whom are you meant to be a healing presence for today?

It has been one of my greatest honours to witness Lisa's transformation as she learned how to become a full embodiment of love, grace, and God's presence. I continue to learn a lot from our experiences together and I always know that when

I reach out for support, I will be met with extraordinary love and acceptance. Lisa's faith and trust in her Divine relationship with God was what inspired me to become a minister also. She taught me that my life is my ministry and I have learned how to embrace and live my life in deep reverence for everyone and everything, everywhere.

I have experienced firsthand what the healing potential of showing up as a loving presence for others offers. It is a gift that just keeps on giving long after the interaction.

Be a loving presence. It sounds so simple, yet it is not always easy. Be love. Live in alignment with love. Be love in action. Be love in silence. Just be love and see what unfolds within and around you. It will transform your relationships and every aspect of your life. Be a loving presence and miracles will be the side effect.

How Do You Show Up As A Healing Presence?

Reading these stories really inspired me because we have so much to learn from each other. I was inspired to invite all my guest authors to share even more of their wisdom with us, so I asked them to answer this question "How do you show up as a healing presence?" and here is what they were inspired to share.

Marilyn

My answer to this question has changed as I continue to grow. A year ago, I would have said I am a healing presence by giving wings through my writing to the wisdom handed me in interviews and in daily life. However, over this past year, I have noticed when I ground myself and listen with my whole being, becoming fully present in the moment, an opportunity for healing is created. It might be words that bubble up from deep within, which I feel led to share, or it might be guidance to simply stand quietly, bearing witness to someone's outpouring. This last was the biggest surprise. I look forward to continuing this journey and expanding how I can be a healing presence in this world.

Kirsten

As I walk my path of life and healing, I have been strengthening my foundation of faith and trust. As this unfolds I am able to show up as a solid presence of peace and love. I see the capacity for myself to heal and be open to hold space and love for myself. This then strengthens my ability to hold space for others. I am in awe with what can come from practising non-judgment in all aspects of one's life. How being open and compassionate to all can shift oneself and others in miraculous ways. I receive such joy from being able to show up as an open ear and heart to witness others' stories. By being open, I allow space to open for others and possibly to spark something deep within them. I show up as myself, my raw unfiltered self—someone who is healing, growing, and remembering the truth of being love and holding love for others.

Nicole

I believe I show up as a healing presence for myself and others by deeply listening and honouring people exactly where they are in each moment. I believe I am able to show up because I am deeply committed to my evolution and healing journey.

Kim

I show up as a healing presence by being a beacon of love, light, and connection. By sparking happiness and vitality.

Rosemary

Being a healing presence means two things to me. First is consciously choosing to hold a frequency such as calmness, love, peace, joy, or light, which then ripples out to impact other people. Each morning I ask Spirit what frequency I am meant to hold for the day. Usually the answer is light, but sometimes it is peace or another frequency.

The second meaning for me is being a reflection of others' light, so that they can see the truth of the light within themselves. I think I do this partly unconsciously, just by being present after having done the work to connect with my own light. I also intentionally reflect this to clients as I connect with them in sessions, both through compassionate words and with the feeling of the unconditional positive regard I hold toward them.

Yolanda

I usually let go of my own control and desires. I ask a higher power to take control of the situation and to guide me in what to do and what to say. To use me as a channel of love, for the highest good of all. I give my full attention to the person I am dealing with, holding space for them, and being present. That means not judging, not wanting to fix the situation, not trying to change anything.

In a practical way with my grandkids, I show up as a healing presence when I am playful, when we dance, sing, and laugh together. Also when I am available to them when they need a hug or a kiss from me, and when I listen carefully to all the stories they share about their days. When at night, before bed, we breathe and pray together and share one thing we are grateful for.

Katherine

When I show up as a healing presence, I become tuned in to the bodily experience of what I feel, where I feel it, and how it feels in my body. I notice I feel easy and free in my body. My energy is flowing freely through me and beyond. It's palpable. I am aware of my Divine power connecting to others in my presence. I feel a heightened connection within myself, and with and for anyone in my company. I notice that those present with me drop into groundedness, and I start tuning into them. I can feel our energies connecting, like a gateway to one another. When this happens, my heart softens, opening, receiving, and giving, and my intuitive sensitivity heightens.

My entire being becomes more receptive, curious, and calm yet very alert. Simultaneously, I feel peaceful and immensely grateful. I am not in my head. Instead, I am in my body and sensing all that's unfolding externally and internally, without judgment. I don't notice the passing of time. It feels very stretched, even eternal. I sense "pure presence," and I see how I'm in a state of being versus doing. I can feel my body, mind, and soul communing with each other. In this place of alignment, I know I, as a healing presence, can hold a safe space for others. I love being in this place of deep, healing presence. It allows me to feel as though I've come home to the heart of who I am and my purpose here on planet earth to love and help others shine their light.

Chela

I show up as Love, no judgment, no criticism—just unconditional Love. It has become a daily practice. When I first began shifting, it was touch and go. I could remain in this state of oneness and love for only a very short amount of time. Now, I can remain here for days at a time and it is wonderful. In fact, when I find myself feeling any separation, I get very uncomfortable and do whatever it is I have to do in order to get back to being at one.

Kelli

I choose to show up as a healing presence in the world by making myself a priority and working on healing myself. I feel the time and years I have invested in healing myself have had a positive impact and healing presence on the people I choose to surround myself with. As I continue to grow and learn more about myself and heal the parts of me that have been wounded, I get to take this information and share it with others. It is very empowering to share the tools that have been life-changing to myself and others. It is a beautiful thing to watch others also do the inner work needed to live a freer life that brings out the kinder, gentler, and more loving person in them.

Miranda

As I consider Sue's final question, I find myself in a rural French village with a group of close friends from around the world—what a wonderful place to contemplate how I show up as a healing presence. I am noticing two distinct areas: first, as a healing presence for others, I feel my approach is quiet and unassuming. I like to listen, observe, and absorb, and offer insights where I can. My deepest intention is to do my best to empathize and strike the right balance between talking and listening to make sure that people feel heard as well as seen. Then, as a healing presence for myself, the balance seems to be between time alone and time with loved ones. When I'm able to place my full attention in the moment and I am free from obligation and the shoulds of life, that presence allows conversations, interactions, and experiences to feed my soul and expand my mind.

Kimberley

I show up as a healing presence in my life by doing my best to stay in alignment with my Divine self while simultaneously honouring my human self, as messy and beautiful as it is at times. I keep my energy grounded and calm so I can support others, and I am committed to shining my light and reminding others to do the same.

Aparna

My fertility journey became an invitation for personal transformation and extraordinary growth in a way that I could never have imagined. It beckoned me to open doors that I had desperately tried to keep shut. I was navigating a myriad of emotions on this landscape, including anger, grief, feeling left behind, cursed, isolated, and shamed. This journey rocked me to my core and stretched me far beyond my comfort limits.

In accepting the path and embracing the ride as it showed up helped me walk in deep trust and blind faith in the Divine. I can only become a healing presence when I have radically accepted myself—both the gifts and the shadow parts alike—which is an ongoing process. This journey has taught me that there is only so much I know about another person's life in a given moment, so, to me, being a healing presence is showing up as an empathic, non-judgmental companion who can walk beside and hold a compassionate space for myself and for others.

Julie

As a book publisher, story coach, and retreat centre host, I inspire people to share their most vulnerable and authentic story, to help heal others by inspiring them and sharing their own healing story. Sharing your story is a very healing experience, on so many levels. It heals the person who is exploring their own life story to understand their own healing journey, and it inspires those who receive the story to look at their own healing journey through their life story. I am the healer's healer by encouraging the storyteller to dig deeper, embrace vulnerability, and conquer the ego that wants to portray only the strengths and hide the weaknesses and traumas. Sharing at this level takes courage as most people are in fear of judgment; but in reality, stories at this level of vulnerability are very healing for other people to read, to know that they are not alone in their own fears.

April

The theme of my life now is freedom. I am here for my freedom. So how do I show up as a healing presence? By simply showing up, as I am. In living my life in its fullest expression, I allow others a taste of their own freedom by touching a little corner of mine.

It would be selfish for me to keep a good thing to myself. I am a promoter of healers and health practitioners, alternative therapies, and all the woo-woo stuff! I am a bridge between the corporate and the intuitives. I am a connector of like-minded people. I am an initiator, activator, and a community builder. I help a new breed of entrepreneurs launch soulful businesses—the Intuitive Entrepreneurs.

My dream is to live in a world where we can live in harmony and embrace our intuitive gifts. Where the rebels, the edge dwellers, the free thinkers, and the black sheep of the family can be seen as beacons of light instead of as the bad apples. So I am here to encourage all the undercover mystics to help heal the world by supporting them as their guide and intuitive business coach.

I expect miracles to happen every day—and they do!

Jacky

I am not sure how to answer the question of how I show up as a healing presence. It's not like I am consciously coaching myself to BE a healing presence. I am simply doing my best every day, and it's okay if I do not meet my own expectations. I try to feel grounded as much as I can, so that I experience what's happening in the moment, and in a way that allows me to more authentically honour where I am and realize what I need. I simply do my best. For example, sometimes I meditate, sometimes I don't, and I do not beat myself up when I don't start the "perfect spiritual day." When I do meditate, I thank myself for taking myself there. I believe that from that place I can better contribute to the world, in my own unique way.

Kristen

Showing up as a healing presence is about being myself, centred in my heart and being fully present in my awareness. When I am being myself in my heart, centered and present, then my body and mind are relaxed, creating the ability to communicate clearly with others and my surroundings.

Relaxed communication then opens powerful potential for being in the moment and knowing, flowing with, what exactly is needed. This creates a potent field of resonance that allows more transformation, fun, play, and coherent structure for all to come into harmony. No matter what is happening, it is embraced with clarity and love.

Healing for me is when we enter the space of love that is eternal and we can be ourselves in open communication in any situation.

Kevin

I've had this belief for years that I if I continued to raise my frequency I would be able to show up in my highest evolution for myself and others. The more I raised my vibrational field, the more grounded, clear, and loving I would feel. I also believe that when I am in a loving vibration and, ideally, as unconditional as possible, then that energy and frequency are what can bring about a similar energy in others, which ultimately leads to healing.

Observing my patients and clients as rays of light from a central sun bursting with infinite potential helps me assist them in opening the possibilities that were previously forgotten. The body is capable of healing with the right conditions, and we get to create this together as a community. Keeping this deep inner knowing steadfast and fully present, listening to all elements in form and the formless, are how a healing presence can come into being.

Surya

Every moment is an opportunity to show up as a healing presence and this might look different depending on the day, person, and situation. I'm not sure it's something I do intentionally; rather it is what I have become and who I am. I seem often to find myself placed in situations where a kind word, a healing hand, or a compassionate presence is needed. Being willing, open, heart centred, and present is all part of it. Holding a space of unconditional love to the best of my ability as a human is also an important piece.

For as long as I can remember, I have prayed each day to be of service, however I am needed and it's always amazing to see what scenarios present themselves each day!

Lisa

To show up as a healing presence, I consistently practise choosing love over fear. When I choose love, I can then extend that love to those around me. I place my trust and faith in my inner teacher to guide my thoughts, words, and actions. As a healing presence, I live an ordinary life. I walk the dog, do the dishes, drive the kids, counsel a client, teach a class, and hang out with friends. But on an inner level, everything I show up for and experience is infused with greater peace, gentleness, and joy.

How Can We All Be More of a Healing Presence?

How we show up in life has an impact on others. In every moment of our life, we are sending out a beacon in the form of an energetic wave that goes out into the world as a message. That message may be one of love or one of fear. It is a silent, invisible transmission sent and received by the world, whether we want it to be so or not.

Most people are unaware of how much of an impact their inner world has on the outer world. Everything we think, do, and feel has an impact that is more far-reaching than we realize. I am not sharing this to fuel fear. I am sharing this to empower everyone to recognize we have much more power, influence, and impact than we realize.

The good news is we can use this in favour of SHIFTing the energy all around us to raise the vibrational frequency within and around us. When we set a clear intention about what message or beacon we want to send out into the world, we can have profound impact and uplift humanity just by our intention and presence. It all starts with our state of BE-ing.

How we are BE-ing sets the frequency of the beacon we transmit.

Ghandi captured it so clearly and beautifully when he encouraged us to "be the change you wish to see in the world."

When all hope feels lost, we can BE a beacon of hope. We others are stuck in fear, we can BE a beacon of Love. We don't even need to speak or do anything; our state of BE-ing on the inside will be felt by others who are outside.

How we are BE-ing impacts everything, everywhere, in every moment, without exception. So let's all pause and ask ourselves the question: "How am I BE-ing?"

How are you BE-ing when you go to the grocery store, when you show up for work, when you are with your family, at social events, in situations of conflict, as you are walking down the street, and in your everyday moments?

How are you BE-ing and how is that impacting the whole of humanity?

How can you be more a healing presence for others?

We need to focus more on BE-ing rather than on doing. We need to practise being in the doing. After all, we are human beings not human doings.

Society puts so much value on doing that we have forgotten how to be. We are so focused on doing the job or getting things done that most people live on autopilot and miss out on the gifts that the present moment holds.

We value thinking more than feeling. We are so busy staying busy, caught up in our heads, that we are disconnected from our hearts. We are just going through the motions and we miss out on the experiences that life offers, because we are not fully present.

Remembering how to "be present" can be a gift for everyone, including you. When we shift our focus from *doing* back to *BE-ing in the doing* we can experience the richness of life in each moment. We can appreciate the beauty all around us and within each of us.

BE-ing is impenetrable. BE-ing is a force that is powerful beyond measure. BE-ing is the key to shifting everything. BE-ing allows you to rise above the battlefield and witness through the lens of compassion mixed with potential and possibility for a new way of BE-ing in relationship to each other.

Making a conscious choice to BE allows us to be fully present to live from our hearts and be full expressions of our true essence, which is Divine love. Who you "BE" in every moment has profound impact.

Who will you BE today?

BE love. BE light. BE Divinity Embodied. BE compassion. BE empathy. BE peace. BE witness. BE a healing presence for all. BE, just BE, and all will be done.

Wake up every morning and set an intention of who you wish to BE today and watch the miracles that unfold in your relationships, interactions, and experiences. I invite you to be a healing presence by being the presence of love, and watch your life change. I promise the side effects will be miracles.

When we all show up as a healing presence, the world as we know it will heal and we will all remember the Truth that we are love, always have been, always will be.

Thank you for taking this journey with us as we embrace the idea that we are ALL healers. I encourage and invite you to take the lessons, insights, and gifts you have received in this book and share them with others. Be the love, be wisdom, be light, be the healer that I know you are.

The world needs you now more than ever. What do you say? Will you BE what the world needs you to BE? Say yes. Just say yes and see what happens.

About Sue Dumais

Sue Dumais is a Global Impact Visionary and Evolutionary Leader answering the call to heal the world. She is a best-selling author, an international speaker, spiritual mentor, a gifted intuitive healer, an ordained minister, and a global voice of HOPE and inspiration for Heart Led Living.

Sue brings the gifts of insight, awareness, and self-empowerment to her global audience, creating a shift in consciousness from head to heart. Her mission is to ignite our hearts to uplift humanity and unify us in love for each other and our planet.

A humanitarian at heart, Sue created the Heart Led Living Foundation to extend love and healing energy as well as emotional and financial support to empower women and girls in Kenya and around the globe.

This is Sue's seventh published book. Her sixth book was published in 2019 called *The Evolution of the Ego: A Journey to*

Unwind Your Ego, Embrace Your Humanness and Embody Your Divinity.

Sue's previous book—*Stand UP Stand OUT Stand STRONG: A 30-Day Guide to Navigate Life When the SHIFT Hits the Fan*—is proving to be the right book at the right time during our shifting times.

Her signature book—*Heart Led Living: When Hard Work Becomes Heart Work*—features the ten heart led principles that are designed to help awaken our innate ability to heal, trust our intuition, lead with our heart, and discover our "YES!" for life.

Through a divine blend of transformational guidance, unique perspectives, and a radically honest approach, Sue fosters deep healing and profound awakenings. She guides others to hear, answer, and trust the highest calling of their heart. Sue is passionate about illuminating the path for others as they discover, embrace, and embody their true heart YES and fulfil their Soul mission.

About the Guest Authors

Marilyn R. Wilson

Marilyn is a freelance writer, published author, speaker, and budding poet with a passion for listening to others share from their heart. Her career began in an unusual way: by answering a Craigslist ad for which she had no qualifications. It was while conducting her first interview that life shifted. Interviewing was what she was meant to do.

Whether through a random encounter or a scheduled interview, her goal is the same—to give wings to the stories of inspiring individuals through magazine articles and books including *Life Outside the Box and The Wisdom of Listening*.

To learn more about Marilyn visit
www.marilynrwilson.com.

Kirsten Jorgensen

Kirsten is curious about life. She is a woman whose path included infertility, which led her to the start of remembrance. That journey opened the doors to a path of self re-discovery and healing, for which she is so grateful. Unlearning has been awakening and freeing, allowing her to reconnect with her heart and inner knowing. This led her to become a certified intuitive coach, and has deepened her trust and faith in herself. She trusted and listened to the guidance and started Peaceful Present Parenting while walking her path as a mother.

Peaceful Present Parenting is a safe space for parents to connect with Kirsten as an intuitive coach, a space where they can express, explore, share, and heal themselves. Kirsten has embraced practising her deeper trust in all areas of her life as a woman, daughter, wife, sister, mother, and nurse. If her story and energy resonate with you and you are a parent wanting to dive deeper into any triggers or upsets you are encountering on your parenting journey, head over to www.peacefulpresentparenting.com for more information.

Nicole McCurdy

Nicole is a mother to three boys, a certified intuitive coach, horse whisperer and listener, sound healer, and the owner and operator of Horse Guided Healing Sanctuary located in Langley, British Columbia. She is passionate about helping humans, animals, and mother Earth, helping guide people back to the place of remembering, and reminding them how to come back to themselves. Nicole finds peace while meditating in nature and being in the presence of animals. She offers one-on-one and group sessions that include the support of her horse partners, as well as meditation and sound healing circles, and intuitive coaching. She recently created a horse-guided healing facilitator training program.

To learn more about Nicole and her herd visit www.horseguidedhealing.ca.

Kim Bergen

Kim is a life-long learner and adventurer who follows her heart. After living a pretty straight path in this life's journey, a fun-free childhood, moving from the prairies to the mountains, travelling around the world, going to university to get a "good" job, getting married, having a daughter, going through a messy divorce, falling in love again, and learning how to listen to her intuition, she is opening to the magic that is all around. Kim is grateful for the little nuggets of learning from her teachers, guides, and mentors.

Rosemary Laurel Messmer

Rosemary is a mom, a Certified Intuitive Healer, and a Registered Clinical Counsellor. She has a private counselling practice located in Vancouver, Canada, where she offers both traditional therapy and intuitive counselling. When Rosemary is not working or hanging out with her kids, you are most likely to find her reading a novel, doing her own healing work, or enjoying a walk in the forest.

To learn more about Rosemary visit www.lightupyourheart.ca.

Yolanda Sarmiento

Yolanda is fondly known by her grandkids as Meme. She was born in Colombia and came with her family to Canada in 1991, looking for a brighter future. Yolanda has three joyous devoted roles: as a mother, a grandmother, and a teacher. One of her favourite roles is being a grandma. Yolanda has two beautiful grandchildren whom she adores—Mackson and Natalia. They are her biggest teachers in this life and she has dedicated her story especially to them and to all the precious children in the world!

Katherine Labelle

Katherine's spirituality led her to an inspiring career as a contemporary dancer. During her thirty-year-year calling, her compelling artistry carved her name in many hearts. She was known for her choreography, and for her sensitivity to her audience, which carried over to her teaching. She has taught at various universities, including Simon Fraser University's School for the Contemporary Arts, and performed and taught in various communities throughout Canada, New York City, and Russia. She is the recipient of numerous awards, most notably The Floyd S. Chalmers Performing Arts Training Award.

Since adopting her son in 2004, her attention has shifted to a deeper spiritual calling. She began studies in Usui Reiki and became an Azul Conscious Dance Teacher in 2021. Currently, she is studying intuitive coaching with the goal of supporting families raising special needs children. Her overall mission is to advocate for neurodiverse persons to reap the sense of belonging, for which all humans strive.

Chela Hallenbeck

Raised by a single parent and being biracial were stigmas in Laredo, Texas. Chela's experiences of the death of many loved ones solidified her sense of separation in life. With her inability to process emotions and feeling disconnected, she became lost in a world of alcohol abuse and dissociation from self and others. With God's help, Chela raised two daughters on her own. Both are happily married and doing well. In spite of their mother's difficulty with functioning and fitting in, her daughters never once lost respect for Chela. Their unconditional love and support are the driving forces behind Chela's recovery and awakening.

Kelli Taylor

Kelli (@lifeaskellitaylor) is an award-winning acupuncturist and functional nutritionist. She owns a private practice, Elements Wellness Centre in Vancouver, British Columbia. Kelli teaches Yin Yoga for Hormone Balance and facilitates workshops for women's health. Kelli published *Yin Yoga: The Natural Way to Hormone Balance* in 2023.

To learn more about Kelli visit www.lifeaskellitaylor.com.

Miranda MacKelworth

With a natural curiosity and thirst for knowledge, Miranda is a lifelong student with an intense and enduring passion for spirituality, dreamwork, and personal growth. Her formal training includes Integrative Energy Healing certification from Langara College, Usui Reiki, Medical Intuition, and Matrix Energetics. She has also enjoyed countless workshop intensives, including work with Joe Dispenza and Robert Moss. She loves spending time with her husband of thirty-three years, her grown children, family, and a wonderful circle of friends. Miranda finds inspiration in travel, nature, and a recently reignited enthusiasm for photography.

Kimberley Maxwell

Kimberley helps women, who are ready to rise, to transform their fear into trust, overwhelm into clarity, and stress into calm so that they feel empowered to live a life that is aligned with their truth and led by their Soul. She is dedicated to offering unique and powerful healing experiences and mentorship programs for women to expand their intuitive heart, elevate their Inner Self, and inspire unity.

As an Intuitive Coach, Energy Guide, Reiki Practitioner, Meditation Instructor, mentor, healer, and mother, Kimberley helps to create space within so those she works with can fully embrace who they came here to be.

To learn more about Kimberley visit
https://intuitiveheartsunite.com.

Aparna Vemula

Aparna is a certified Intuitive Coach, Spirit Baby Whisperer, Usui Reiki Master, and a Soul Realignment™ Practitioner. A former microbiologist, she found herself on a long conception journey that became one of self-discovery and deep transformation. Aparna blends her unique intuitive and creative gifts to support women in letting go of old, disempowering stories that have mired them down for years so they can feel lighter and experience more joy and aliveness in their life. She explores the energies of spirit babies in her work to support other women who are experiencing challenging fertility journeys.

To learn more about Aparna visit
https://whisperwithin.me.

Julie Ann

Julie is the founder of Influence Publishing and the author of *Around the World in Seven Years: A Life-Changing Journey*. She specializes in collaborative book projects featuring fifteen to twenty authors, including nine books in the Woman of Worth Series. Influence has published over two hundred books in the last twelve years and made most of them Amazon Best Sellers.

Julie is the host of the podcast show, "House of Influence." She has been the keynote at many conferences, and her 2017 TEDx titled "The Gift of Dyslexia" and has more than 100,000 views on YouTube. She is the owner of the cultural retreat center called Casa de Influencia in Puerto Vallarta.

To learn more about Julie visit
www.influencepublishing.com.

April May Bellia

April is an intuitive guide and a life purpose coach. She enjoys the freedom lifestyle and is a serial entrepreneur. April was the founder of AprilCakes (from 2000-12) and The Granola Girl (2011-21). After exiting her business a couple years ago, April now enjoys living part time in Europe. She specializes in leading women's urban retreats called Les Voyageuses in France and Greece. April continues to coach and help other people launch their soulful businesses through her three-month program called The Optimystic Entrepreneur. Nothing makes April happier than seeing her friends and clients live with passion and feel fully aligned to their Truth and Purpose.

To learn more about April visit https://aprilmaybellia.com.

Jacky A. Yenga

Originally from Cameroon, Central Africa, Jacky grew up in Yaoundé and Paris, and now lives in Vancouver, British Columbia. Founder of the Spirit of the Village, she is a performer, a TEDx speaker, a best-selling author, a cultural medium, and a messenger for the healing wisdom of African villages. She teaches how to use the power of rhythm and movement for healing and wellbeing, and to access joy, align with Source, increase satisfaction, and experience belonging.

To learn more about Jacky visit www.jackyyenga.com.

Kristen Bielecki

Kristen is a Soul Embodiment Guide, Crystalline Grid Architect, Intuitive, and Energy Healer. Through several years of conscious awakening and activations, she now facilitates transformation on all levels of one's being to harmonize Mind, Body, Heart and Soul. She facilitates one into their deep inner awareness of Self to be empowered and divinely guided to live a Soul embodied life to create the New Earth. She has a seven-year-old son and together they love crystals, gardening, and going on adventures!

To learn more about Kristen visit www.awakenedsoul.net.

Kevin Preston

Dr. Kevin Preston trained in Traditional Chinese Medicine, with a background in science and kinesiology. He has spent years branching out from that foundation through many different courses, seminars, and philosophies, ranging from epigenetics, biological medicine, homeopathy, and Classical Chinese Medicine, to other teachings from more esoteric lineages and spiritual paths.

He continues to be inspired by new discoveries in health, and the convergence of modern cutting-edge research with ancient practices and the potential that that holds for humanity's evolution in this new Golden Age. Currently, Dr. Preston is enjoying mentoring, leading healing retreats and events, building courses, and expanding his clinical practice in Vernon, British Columbia.

To learn more visit https://drkevinpreston.com.

Surya Devi

Surya is a long-time practitioner and student of the healing arts. For over twenty years, she has worked with individuals and groups from all walks of life. She is also a world music artist who has released four full length albums plus numerous singles in collaboration with artists from a variety of genres. Her purpose is to serve during the awakening of humanity and her vision is a world that is peaceful, balanced, and prosperous for all.

To learn more about Surya visit https://suryadeviworld.com.

Reverend Lisa Windsor

Reverend Lisa is an ordained spiritual minister, spiritual coach, and *A Course in Miracles* mentor. She founded Modern Miracles Spiritual Wellness, a growing community based on the teachings of *A Course in Miracles*. Lisa has been a student of spirituality for over twenty years and is passionate about living the transformational teachings from ACIM through the practice of true forgiveness. Her deep trust in her Inner Teacher has led to profound healing and clarity. Her approach is focused on practical application and open-hearted honesty. Through the teachings of *A Course in Miracles*, Lisa reveals the miracles that occur when we follow our inner guidance and truly forgive.

Lisa lives near Vancouver, British Columbia, with her four amazing kids who inspire her to forgive often and love unconditionally.

To learn more about Lisa visit www.modernmiracles.com.